The Rise Begins at ZERO

SHABEENA MIRZA

BlueRose ONE .com
Stories Matter
NewDelhi • London

BLUEROSE PUBLISHERS
India | U.K.

For permissions requests or inquiries regarding this publication, please contact:

BLUEROSE PUBLISHERS
www.BlueRoseONE.com
info@bluerosepublishers.com
+91 8882 898 898
+4407342408967

ISBN: 978-93-7139-199-3

Cover design: Yash Singhal
Typesetting: Namrata Saini

First Edition: August 2025

Author's Note

The Rise Begins at Zero

The Rise Begins at Zero was not written from a place of perfection-it was born in the middle of figuring things out.

From the quiet in-betweens. The foggy days. The doubts I didn't say out loud.

From the rewrites, the setbacks, and the small, tired wins no one saw.

This is not a guide full of answers. It is a reflection of the journey-yours and mine.

It is for the ones who have felt like they are running behind.

For the ones who have questioned if they are ever going to get it "right."

For the ones who are still trying–softly, quietly, but consistently.

If you have ever wondered whether your efforts matter,

If you have ever felt invisible in your own progress,

I hope *The Rise Begins at Zero* helps you see the strength in simply staying in the game.

You don't have to be loud to be powerful.

You don't have to be fearless to move forward.

And just in case no one's told you lately–

I am proud of you.

For being here.

For holding on.

For beginning, again.

Let's take this next step together.

–Shabeena Mirza

Acknowledgment

This book was never mine alone—it is stitched together from countless moments that shaped me—late nights spent wrestling with half-formed ideas, mornings when a single line felt like progress, and the quiet in-betweens where doubt sat heavier than hope. It belongs just as much to the journeys of the people whose stories, struggles, and quiet triumphs live within these pages.

It grew out of messy drafts, hesitant beginnings, and the slow process of finding clarity, one sentence at a time. Each false start, each tiny breakthrough, and each pause to simply breathe became part of its making.

The blank page often felt impossible, yet the act of showing up—again and again—taught me that creating is less about certainty and more about persistence.

Every chapter holds pieces of lessons learned, mistakes made, and the quiet courage to try anyway.

To every reader who finds a reflection of their own journey here—you are the reason these words matter. May they feel like a steady presence reminding you, "You are not alone."

This book is proof that beginnings can be messy, slow, and full of doubt–and still lead to something worth holding on to.

With all my heart,

Shabeena

Keywords:

Inspiration for youth • Anyone Starting from scratch • Real talk for Gen Z • Goal setting • Self-belief • Personal growth • No more waiting • Rise from zero • Purpose and passion • Motivation that sticks • Shabeena Mirza • Youth empowerment

Dedication

For the ones who are still trying–

even when it's hard,

even when no one's clapping,

even when the path ahead feels unclear.

This is for you.

For the dreamers sitting quietly at the back,

the overthinkers with full hearts and shaky starts,

the ones who have had to begin again–more than once.

You are not behind. You are becoming.

And for the younger version of me,

the one who questioned her voice, her pace, her place.

I hope you would be proud of how far we have come.

This book is a reminder that rising doesn't always look like winning.

Sometimes, it just looks like not giving up.

This is for every soul still choosing to show up.

You are not alone. You never were.

And you never will be again—not with these pages in your hands.

This book is also dedicated to everyone who helped me learn something—

whether through kindness, challenge, or quiet support.

To those who shaped my journey, knowingly or not.

Some of you are too special to be named,

but know this: a piece of your wisdom lives here too.

—Shabeena Mirza

"Sometimes the bravest thing you can do is just keep showing up."

—Unknown

Description

She left behind everything she knew-her country, her comfort, her sense of belonging, with nothing but a single bag and a storm of shattered dreams. Her heart beat with hope, but her path was a blur. There was no roadmap. No familiar voices. Just a restless spirit clinging to the belief that somewhere, somehow, a better life was waiting.

The Weight of One Bag

She left with less than most could bear–
Not just things, but a life left there.
A language tucked behind her teeth,
A street that slept beneath her feet.
The voices gone, the daily ways,
Now traded for uncertain days.
She knocked on doors that stayed shut tight,
Swallowed her pride to sleep at night.
In quiet rooms that didn't care,
She stitched her wounds with silent prayer.
No guide, no map, just faith so thin–
But still, she stood. She let life in.
Not all fresh starts are bold and bright.
Some take their shape in lonely nights.
But little by little, loss gave way–
To strength, to grit, to finding stay.
And though the past still gently sighs,
She's building now, beneath new skies.
For even broken wings can glide,
And build a life on the other side.

When she stepped onto foreign soil, she was utterly alone-lost in translation, drowning in doubt, and overwhelmed by the unknown. The silence was deafening. The fears were real. The future felt like a blank page, too heavy to write on. But she kept moving—step by step, tear by tear, lesson by lesson.

She didn't just rebuild her life—she rebuilt herself.

From invisible to unstoppable.

From uncertain to unshakable.

Her rise didn't begin with certainty. It began with courage. It began at zero.

She was not always driven—there were days she felt lazy, unmotivated, and unsure. But what never wavered was her willpower. Deep down, she knew that this new opportunity could only be cracked with sheer determination.

And it is stories like hers that breathe life into these pages—stories that are raw, real, and a testament to the power of starting from absolutely nothing.

"She Kept Showing Up"

She didn't rise like fireworks do–
No spark, no crowd, no perfect cue.
Just messy starts and tired eyes,
And mornings chasing cloudy skies.
She doubted more than she believed,
But still showed up, still didn't leave.
Some days she sat, too numb to try,
But even then, she didn't lie–
To the voice inside that softly said,
"You're not done yet. Get out of bed."
No magic switch, no sudden light,
Just small brave steps into the fight.
She built a life from scattered bits,
From quiet wins and awkward fits.
Not flawless-just fiercely true.
She didn't need a map-she moved.

This book is not about perfection. It is about permission.

The permission to be messy. To begin unsure. To rise anyway.

This is not just another motivational book filled with clichés and success stories told from mountaintops. *The Rise Begins At Zero* is written from the valley—from the place where the air is heavy, the road is unclear, and the dream still feels too fragile to name out loud.

It is for every person who has looked at their life and whispered, "I imagined I would have made more progress by now."

It is for those who feel like the late bloomers, the outsiders, the underdogs, the ones who have been underestimated—not just by the world, but by themselves.

It is for the ones who had to start over—because of loss, heartbreak, migration, failure, burnout, or simply because life didn't go the way they planned.

Author Shabeena Mirza writes with soul-deep honesty and a voice that feels like a trusted friend—the kind who doesn't sugar-coat, but also never lets you give up on yourself.

She speaks to the *young dreamer* standing at life's starting line. The *quiet creative* whose voice has been buried under noise. The *ambitious misfit* who wants more, even when the world tells them to settle.

She knows what it is like to scroll through everyone else's success stories and wonder if your turn will ever come.

She knows what it is like to feel left behind while others sprint ahead.

She knows what it is like to rebuild not just goals—but a sense of self.

And now, she's passing on every lesson, every breakthrough, and every truth she wished someone had told her when she was at zero.

She didn't always feel strong—but she showed up anyway.

Willpower wasn't loud, it was quiet and stubborn.

And that's what carried her through.

This book is your mirror, your map, and your momentum.

In *The Rise Begins At Zero*, you'll discover:

- Why waiting to feel "ready" is the enemy of progress
- How to start scared, but start anyway
- Why discipline will always outlast motivation
- How to lead yourself when no one else shows up

- How to stop waiting for permission, praise, or the "perfect" moment
- The power of silence, focus, and cutting the noise
- How to trust yourself even when you feel unqualified
- The truth about resilience, confidence, and why self-trust is built, not gifted

Through practical chapters, real-world reflections, and powerful journaling prompts, this book doesn't just talk about rising—it helps you *do it.*

Every chapter closes with raw questions, nudging you inward—into the places where transformation really begins.

This is not a book about success.

It is a book about *starting.*

Because you don't need a five-year plan to begin.

You just need one brave decision-to move.

Why now?

Because we are living in an age of overwhelm.

Too many voices. Too much pressure. Too little real connection.

We scroll, compare, and consume. But we rarely pause long enough to *hear ourselves.*

To ask, *What do I really want?*

Who do I want to be?

And why am I waiting?

This book is a reset. A breath. A reclaiming of your timeline.

It reminds you that you are not too late.

That your dreams are still alive, even if they have been quiet.

That your story doesn't need to be perfect—it just needs to be yours.

You won't find magic formulas here.

But you will find:

- Permission to begin again
- A voice that doesn't talk down to you—but walks beside you
- Stories that sound a lot like yours—full of doubt, hope, missteps, and quiet victories
- Reminders that every single person you admire... started at zero too

You will meet Bina and others whose journeys are gently woven throughout the book—composites of real emotions, real struggles, and the kind of silent strength found in everyday people like you and me. She's the reflection of so many of us who dared to begin even when it didn't make sense on paper. Her moments of hesitation, her quiet breakthroughs, her imperfect steps—they are anchors for anyone who's ever asked, "Can I really do this?"

Spoiler: Yes, you can.

So if you have ever...

- Felt like you are behind in life
- Struggled to believe in yourself
- Been paralyzed by fear or perfectionism
- Waited for the "right time" that never came
- Wondered if starting over was even worth it

...this book was written for you.

Not to impress you. But to remind you:

You are not alone.

You are not too late.

You are not broken.

You're just at zero.

And zero is a beginning—never an end.

"Where It All Begins"

It didn't start with confidence—
It started with a mess.
With late nights, heavy thoughts,
And a heart that whispered "yes."
You didn't have a blueprint,
Just a bruise or two and hope.
You took the first unsure step,
And called that courage just to cope.
It wasn't magic, wasn't clean-
You stumbled, paused, and cried.
But every time you showed back up,
Something stronger grew inside.
And maybe no one saw it,
But you kept moving all the same.
That quiet fight to keep on trying?
That's how you earn your name.
You don't rise when you're ready.
You rise when you stop waiting.
You rise when you choose to move—even if you're trembling.
You rise when you say:
"I don't have it all figured out. But I am not staying here."
Let The Rise Begins At Zero be your permission slip.
Your nudge.

Your next page.

Your power.

Because the truth is:

You don't have to start strong.

You just have to start.

Contents

Introduction

By Shabeena Mirza

Let me start with a simple truth:

Most people don't start at the top. They start at zero.

No fancy background. No support system. No secret blueprint. Just questions, doubts, and maybe a dream too fragile to say out loud. If that sounds familiar–you're in the right place.

Zero isn't failure. It's potential. It's the place where all great journeys begin.

Think of it like potential energy–it looks like nothing is happening, but trust me, the moment you take that first step, gravity (or life) kicks in and you're suddenly in motion.

I have always wanted to write something real. Not sugar-coated inspiration, not recycled advice–but something that actually speaks to the young person who is figuring things out. The one scrolling through everyone else's "success" stories and wondering if they'll ever get there.

This book is for you.

For the one who keeps trying, even if nobody claps.

For the one who feels like time is slipping away.

For the one who is just tired—but still hoping.

Here's what I have learned: the rise doesn't begin with having all the answers. It begins the moment you stop waiting for the perfect moment. It begins when you decide that even starting from scratch is better than standing still.

And yes, zero can feel overwhelming. It's that place where your bank account, confidence, or direction all feel equally empty. But zero is also a clean slate. It's the place where you stop chasing what others expect and start building something real for yourself.

In the chapters ahead, I am not promising overnight success. But I will walk with you. I will share what helped me move forward when I had no map. We will talk about fear, failure, habits, purpose—everything I wish someone had sat me down and said, "Hey, it's okay.

If you have been waiting for a sign—this is it.

Not because I wrote it, but because you're still reading.

Because deep down, something in you refuses to give up.

So, let's do this.

Let's start at zero—and rise.

From quiet falls and honest pain.

Each stumble taught what strength can't fake,

We break, we build, we rise—we make.

But before we rise, let's be honest.

You might be feeling stuck, lost, or even invisible. You might be in a place where it feels like everyone around you is moving forward—getting promotions, degrees, weddings, dream homes—while you are still figuring out what direction to even walk in.

I know that feeling. I've lived it.

There were moments I sat alone, staring at a blank screen, wondering if I had missed my chance. But even in the silence, I never let regret consume me. I knew I'd made mistakes-some big, some careless, but I chose to see them as lessons, not failures. Every wrong move showed me something I hadn't seen before. And with each one, I got a little closer to making things right, in my own time, in my own way.

Moments where I questioned every choice that brought me to that point.

Moments where I thought, "*Maybe I am just not cut out for more.*"

But here's something no one told me then—and what I want to tell you now:

You are not behind.

You are not broken.

You are just at the beginning.

And beginnings are powerful.

See, we glorify the finish line. We celebrate the glow-ups, the success reels, the polished resumes. But we forget the mess behind them—the doubts, the bad days, the quiet wins no one noticed. And if no one's told you this yet: that messy middle? That quiet, unsure beginning? That's where the magic actually happens.

I knew someone who used to sit in the corner of a noisy café every night after work. She didn't look like she had it all figured out—tired eyes, chipped nail polish, a second-hand laptop that overheated if she opened too many tabs. She was juggling two jobs and night classes, barely making rent, and trying to teach herself something new just to feel like she wasn't stuck.

There was no big plan, no clear path—just a quiet kind of hope and a messy kind of effort. She applied for jobs and didn't hear back. She got things wrong, failed a few courses, and had more breakdowns than breakthroughs. But she kept showing up. Kept trying.

A year later, she got an entry-level role doing exactly what she'd been working toward. No spotlight. No big applause. Just a quiet moment alone in that same café, letting it sink in that she'd made it through.

That's the part we don't talk about enough—the middle. The part where you are unsure, unseen, but still showing up. That's where the real magic lives. That's where the rise begins.

This book was born from the belief that someone needs to speak to the person *before* the TED Talk. *Before* the success story. *Before* the "I made it" Instagram post.

To the person who is just trying to get out of bed and believe in themselves again.

Maybe you are starting after a major setback.

Maybe you are pivoting from something you thought would work out.

Maybe life didn't unfold the way you planned.

Maybe you are just tired of waiting—for permission, for the right moment, for someone to notice.

Wherever you are right now, you're not alone.

And I want to make you a promise.

This book won't pretend to fix everything. It won't give you a perfect five-step plan. But it will hold your hand through the hard questions. It will sit with you in the quiet moments. And it will gently push you forward when fear tries to freeze you.

Because I have been there too.

The doubt, the silence, the starting over, I have walked that road, and you are not walking it alone.

I know what it's like to build something from nothing. To be the only one cheering for yourself. To walk into rooms where no one knows your name—and make space anyway. I know what it's like to cry in the shower, then show up to work like everything's fine. I know what it's like to feel like you are running out of time—when, in fact, you're just warming up.

This is not about chasing someone else's version of success.

It's about finding what *matters to you*—and daring to build a life around it.

In this book, you will find stories. Real ones. Some from my life. Some inspired by countless conversations I have had with dreamers, doers, and quiet warriors who started with nothing but a stubborn belief that they were meant for more. You'll meet people who were scared, unsure, broken, or burnt out-and still moved anyway.

You'll meet someone who worked night shifts while building a dream during the day.

Someone who applied to ten jobs and heard nothing back-until the eleventh changed everything.

Someone who spent years playing it safe before finally taking the leap-and landing somewhere better than they imagined.

You'll see parts of yourself in these pages.

And more importantly, I hope you'll start to see what's *possible* for you.

I am not here to talk at you.

I am here to talk *with* you.

Because you don't need more noise. You need honesty. You need a reminder that it's okay to not have it all figured out. That it's okay to move slowly. That it's okay to feel scared and still start anyway.

This book is permission.

To begin again.

To redefine what success means.

To choose yourself.

To stop waiting and start building.

To trust your voice, even when it shakes.

So, when you turn the page and dive into Chapter One, I want you to know this:

You are not reading a motivational speech.

You are reading a love letter to your starting point.

To your zero.

Because zero doesn't mean empty. It means open. ***In physics terms, it's like absolute zero—everything seems still, but hidden energy and potential can still exist in ways you can't yet see.***

Open to learning. Open to growing. Open to becoming.

This is your moment.

Not next year. Not after you fix everything. Not when you're "more ready."

Right now. As you are.

Because *The Rise Begins at Zero*—and you have already taken the first step just by picking up this book. ***If life feels like Newton's first law right now—that you'll stay stuck unless something gives you a push—let this book be that small force that finally gets you moving.***

Let's walk together from here.

Let's turn the doubt into direction.

Let's rise—not because we have it all together—but because we are finally done waiting.

So take a breath.

You are not behind. You're not alone.

You are just getting started.

So, let's start at zero—and let's rise.

And somewhere, not too long ago, someone just like you did exactly that.

He arrived in the city with nothing but a plastic bag, a stitched-up dream, and a borrowed faith in himself.

No money.

No contacts.

No backup plan.

Just hope—and hunger, both literal and metaphorical.

He slept on station platforms. Cold floors. Public benches.

He bathed at railway taps.

Used a folded shirt as a pillow.

Ate whatever he could afford—or skipped meals when he couldn't.

With an MSc and B.Ed in his pocket, he started applying for jobs-anything that could get him back on his feet.

One day, he got a call for an interview.

He walked for miles in the sun, heart quietly pounding with possibility.

He cleaned his shoes the best he could. Pressed his only shirt. Sat up straight.

But when he reached and introduced himself, the head of security looked at him, surprised.

He smiled kindly and said,

"Sir, with your qualifications... this job isn't meant for you."

It was for a watchman's position.

Not a teacher. Not an academic. Just a post that would pay something.

He didn't respond with pride or ego—just a quiet nod and a heavy heart.

It wasn't the work he couldn't do. It was the knowledge that he had worked too hard for too long to feel this unseen.

Still, he didn't stop.

He applied to every school, coaching centre, and learning institute he could find.

Day after day, application after application.

It was like building momentum—every rejection felt like friction slowing him down, but each attempt still added a little more force to his journey

Most didn't reply. Some rejected him outright.

"You don't have the experience."

"We are looking for someone else."

"You are overqualified."

The rejections stung—but they didn't break him.

And then, one day, something shifted.

One of those very institutions that had turned him away?

They called him back.

What changed?

Weeks passed after the string of rejections. He had knocked on so many doors that he'd lost count. One of them was a respected educational institute, a place where he had applied multiple times. His CV had been dismissed, probably without even being read properly.

But life, as it often does, had its own quiet plans.

The head of the institute who had earlier rejected him resigned from his post. A new head stepped in, someone with a different perspective, perhaps more open, more grounded.

As the new head settled in, he began reviewing old files, clearing out drawers, and going through unattended applications.

And that's when he saw it—tucked away in a dusty corner of an old folder—**his** application.

No recommendation attached. No influence. Just raw qualifications and an honest cover letter.

Something about it caught his eye.

He picked up the phone and dialled the number listed.

That call changed everything.

The same place that had once said "no" now wanted to meet him.

Not because he chased them down again, but because his persistence had waited silently for the right moment.

Because destiny doesn't always arrive with fanfare, it sometimes walks in quietly, through a change in leadership or a shift in timing.

And just like that, the door that once felt permanently shut... opened.

He didn't walk in feeling triumphant. He walked in humbled—but ready.

Sometimes, like in physics, nothing seems to happen until you reach that critical threshold—then suddenly, the "reaction" begins.

He hadn't given up when the world looked the other way.

And that made all the difference.

This is how destiny works.

Not always loud.

Not always fast.

But always fair—to those who keep showing up, even when it feels pointless.

Because sometimes, the "no" you receive today... is just a "not yet" waiting to become a "yes" in the hands of time.

Because real beginnings don't always come wrapped in applause.

Sometimes they come disguised as rejection.

Sometimes they whisper instead of roar.

But they come—for those who keep showing up.

If you are facing your own string of "no's" right now, let this be a reminder:

You are not invisible.

You are not behind.

You are building something that the world hasn't seen yet.

Just keep walking.

Even when the road is silent.

Even when the job is not what you hoped for.

Because one day, the world will look back and say:

"He started with nothing—and still made it."

And so will you.

Some stories don't begin with certainty, they begin with surrender.

And for many, like the man with the plastic bag and stitched-up dreams, the real shift doesn't happen all at once.

It begins in quiet moments. In setbacks that sting. In rejections that feel personal.

But somewhere in the middle of all that chaos, something clicks.

And that–

That is the wake-up call.

In the noise, when hope feels thin,

You breathe once deep and start again.

No spotlight shines, no crowd will cheer,

But something stirs and silences fear.

That spark inside? It kept you here.

The Journey Ahead

These are not just chapters–they are milestones, reminders, and quiet turning points tucked between pages.

A path carved through hesitation, doubt, restarts, and quiet courage.

Each chapter was written for the moments when you felt like giving up, questioning your worth, or starting from scratch-again.

These pages won't promise perfection, but they will offer perspective.

So take what you need, skip around if you like, and come back when life feels loud.

This journey is yours now. Let's walk it together.

Chapter 1
The Wake-Up Call

The moment when something clicks—and everything begins to shift.

Let's be honest: most wake-up calls are not dramatic. They are not movie scenes. There is no thunderclap, no one shouting "You are made for more!"

Sometimes, it is a quiet moment—like scrolling through your phone at 2 AM and realizing you have spent the last five hours watching other people live their lives... while yours is still on pause.

Sometimes, it's looking in the mirror and realizing you have been surviving, not living.

And sometimes, it's hearing someone say something ordinary that hits different:

"You have got more in you than this."

That moment? That is your wake-up call.

Kind of like physics—nothing moves until you apply a force. You're basically a lazy object at rest saying, "Nope, not today." The second you give yourself a tiny push? Bam- Newton would be proud

The Trap of "Someday"

A lot of us grow up with this unspoken idea:

"I will do something amazing... someday."

But here is the thing: someday is not a day. It's a delay.

We wait for the perfect plan, perfect timing, perfect mindset. But life doesn't work like that. The perfect moment rarely comes. Most people don't rise because they are waiting to feel ready. And truthfully? You might never feel ready.

Think of it like waiting for 'ideal conditions' in a physics lab—perfect temperature, perfect pressure, perfect alignment. Reality check? If scientists waited for perfect conditions, we'd still be rubbing sticks to make fire.

I used to believe I needed more: more clarity, more money, more approval. But all I really needed was to stop waiting and start. Even if I stumbled. Even if I started small. Especially if I started scared.

Because real growth begins the moment you say, "I can't keep waiting for someday."

Here is what's wild: even when we feel stuck, life is still moving. Time is passing. Opportunities are floating by. We say no to them not out of disinterest, but out of doubt. We think:

- What if I fail?

- What will people say?
- What if I am not ready?

But what if you are?

What if the version of you five years from now is begging you to just start today?

The difference between where you are and where you want to be isn't a miracle. It's a decision. Not to do everything. Just something.

Why You Feel Stuck

Feeling stuck isn't laziness. It's often fear pretending to protect you.

- Fear of failing
- Fear of judgment
- Fear of starting and realising you are not good enough

But here's the secret: you grow through action, not overthinking.

The more you do, the more you learn. The more you try, the braver you become.

Stuck is not permanent, it is a sign something inside you wants to move.

Being stuck is like kinetic friction—you're not moving because fear is that rough surface under you. But once you push past it, momentum kicks in and everything feels easier. Until then, you're basically that box in

every physics problem that refuses to budge while the student screams, "JUST MOVE ALREADY!"

Being stuck is like being parked at a green light. You know you can go. You want to go. But you keep your foot on the brake because the road looks scary.

Eventually, you get tired of watching everyone else drive by. And that fatigue? That restlessness? That uncomfortable tension?

That's your soul telling you: it's time.

A Wake-Up Call in Real Life

Take one example.

Someone spent three years stuck in a job that drained them. They convinced themselves it was "secure" and "safe." Every day felt the same. Wake up, log in, zone out.

One night, after a particularly draining meeting, they overheard a stranger in a café say, "You either build your dream or get hired to build someone else's."

It wasn't said to them. But it struck like lightning.

They went home and opened a notebook they had buried in a closet–the one filled with business ideas and passion projects they never dared to start.

That night, they didn't launch a company or quit their job. But they did make one small decision: to stop postponing themselves. To stop pressing snooze on their potential.

That was their wake-up call. Quiet. Ordinary. But life-changing.

Your wake-up call might not look the same. It might be triggered by a moment of frustration. Or a glimpse of someone else doing what you wish you were brave enough to do.

It might be a breakup. A breakdown. Or just a breakdown in your daily routine that makes you question everything.

It could even be this page, this very moment, whispering: *Wake up. It's your time.*

You miss a call,

burn the toast,

forget what day it is—

and somehow,

everything feels off.

You sit a little longer

at the edge of the bed,

not tired,

just... unsure

how to move.

It's not a crisis,

not really.

Just a quiet ache—

like your life is

gently asking

if this is still

what you want.

The Myth of the Grand Moment

We are conditioned by movies and stories to expect transformation to be dramatic. We think we need a defining moment, a big break, or a miracle. But most real change begins in the small, almost forgettable decisions.

It begins when you:

- Choose to stop complaining and start researching.
- Say no to one more thing that doesn't serve you.
- Write the first page, send the first email, take the first walk.

You might not even notice the moment when your life begins to shift.

But one day, you will look back and realize: that was the moment. That is when I started rising.

This Is Your Moment

If you are reading this and nodding even a little bit, then consider this your moment. Your real, no-drama, perfectly quiet wake-up call.

It doesn't need to be loud to change your life.

You just have to decide that today is better than someday. That now is good enough.

That you can rise—not after everything is perfect, but right now, even from zero.

You don't have to quit your job or uproot your life overnight. Sometimes, the first step is internal:

- A shift in belief.
- A decision to start valuing yourself.
- A promise to stop waiting for approval.

You don't need clarity. You need courage.

You don't need guarantees. You need grit.

Because this world doesn't need more perfect people. It needs more real people. People willing to try, to fail, to get back up. People who rise, not because it's easy, but because something in them says, "I can't stay here anymore."

From Numb to Noticing

For some of us, the wake-up call is simply a return to feeling. We have been so numb for so long, going through the motions, smiling at the right times, saying "I am fine" when we are anything but.

Then something small breaks through. A book. A quote. A tear. A deep breath.

And suddenly, we are aware again.

Aware that we have been settling.

Aware that life has more in store for us.

Awareness is the first spark. But action is the flame.

So, if you're here, reading this, already feeling the flicker of something inside–don't turn away. Don't put the book down and promise yourself you will come back later.

Start now. Even if it is just writing one line in a notebook:

"This is where I begin."

Because you don't need to wait for a dramatic moment to rise. You just need to *notice* the moment you are already in.

And choose.

To wake up.

To move.

To rise.

Reflection & Journal Page

For Chapter 1: The Wake-Up Call

Your Wake-Up Moment

What part of this chapter hit home for you? Write it down. Circle it. Sit with it.

→ What moment in your life felt like a quiet wake-up call?

What is Holding You Back?

Fear? Self-doubt? Waiting for the "right time"? Be honest—nobody else is reading this.

→ What is the #1 reason you haven't started yet?

Tiny Step, Big Shift

Progress doesn't begin with a giant leap. It starts with a tiny, stubborn decision.

→ What one small action can you take today to move forward-no matter how small?

Self-Talk Reboot

Write one sentence that you will tell yourself whenever doubt creeps in. Make it strong. Make it real.

→ **Your new mantra:**

"I may be starting from zero, but..."

Chapter 2
The Lie of Laziness

What if you are not lazy at all? What if you are just tired, overwhelmed, or quietly afraid?

Let's be real.

We have all had days where we couldn't get ourselves to move.

Not because we didn't care.

But because everything felt heavy—our thoughts, our bodies, our expectations.

It's basically Newton's first law in action—too much "mental mass" makes it hard to move. If Newton were alive today, he'd probably just nod and say, "Yeah, that's inertia... also, same."

So, we scroll. We binge. We avoid.

Then we beat ourselves up for it.

We say, "Ugh, I am so lazy."

But here is the thing-

You are not lazy. You are human.

And being human is hard sometimes.

Even the Earth slows down for a split second every leap second. So if a whole planet takes tiny breaks, you can too.

You are not hopeless because you are not constantly productive.

You are not a failure because you didn't crush your to-do list.

Maybe you are just tired.

Maybe your mind is full.

Maybe you are scared to try again because last time... it didn't work out.

We don't talk enough about that kind of fear—the one that hides behind procrastination.

It is not that you don't want to move forward.

It is that deep down, you are afraid of what happens if you do... and it still doesn't go right.

So, you pause.

You put things off.

You tell yourself you will start "tomorrow."

And then tomorrow feels just as hard.

It's like waiting for "perfect lab conditions" before doing a science experiment. If scientists waited for that, gravity would still just be a rumour.

Sound familiar?

It's okay. Me too.

What's Really Going On?

Sometimes we confuse exhaustion with laziness.

We confuse fear with a lack of motivation.

We confuse burnout with being "unproductive."

But you are *not* your pace.

You are not your unfinished projects.

You are not lazy just because you are overwhelmed.

Think of yourself as a ball at the top of a hill—you're not stuck, you're just storing up potential energy until you're ready to roll. (Hopefully without crashing into anything... but hey, that's life.)

Let's stop pretending laziness is a personality flaw.

Most of the time, it's just a signal.

A whisper from your body or your mind saying: *"Something's off. Please slow down or start differently."*

A Small True Story

There is someone I know who used to call herself lazy all the time.

She would make lists and never check them off. She would watch people chase their goals while she sat on her bed, stuck in her head.

She hated that feeling.

Then one day, instead of forcing herself to be "productive," she asked herself:

"What would feel kind right now?"

Not urgent. Not impressive. Just kind.

That day, she cleaned her desk.

The next day, she lit a candle and wrote one sentence in her journal.

By the end of the week, she would finish a page.

And slowly, she was back in motion—not because she pushed harder, but because she gave herself *grace.*

If You Need to Hear This Today...

You don't need to "fix" yourself.

You don't need to earn your worth through constant doing.

You just need to listen-to your body, your heart, your energy-and start *gently.*

Tiny actions count.

So does resting.

So does *not quitting on yourself*, even if you are moving slowly.

Because you are not lazy.

You are learning how to begin again.

And that's one of the bravest things anyone can do.

Reflection & Journal Page

For Chapter 2: The Lie of Laziness

Be Honest with Yourself

→ When do you tend to call yourself "lazy"? What's really going on in those moments?

Dig Deeper

→ Are you tired? Overwhelmed? Afraid? Burnt out? Write it down–no filter.

A Kind Action

→ What's one small, gentle thing you can do today that feels doable not perfect, just possible?

Rewrite the Script

→ Complete this sentence:

"I am not lazy. I am just..."

Then read it out loud like you mean it.

Chapter 3
Start Scared, But Start

Because waiting to feel ready might mean never starting at all.

Let's get real-starting is scary.

You might have a dream so big it keeps you up at night, but when it comes to actually doing something about it... your mind freezes.

"What if I mess everything up?"

"Will they judge me for stumbling?"

"What if I am just pretending to be capable?"

I have had those thoughts too. More times than I can count. And here's the truth no one tells you: feeling scared doesn't mean you're not ready. It means you're human.

It's like quantum physics–right now, your dream is in "Schrödinger's box." It's both amazing and a total flop at the same time. But the only way to find out? Open the box (a.k.a. actually start). Otherwise, you'll just sit there like Schrödinger's cat, confused and hungry.

Everyone Starts Scared

You are not broken because you are nervous. You are not weak because your hands shake when you speak up, post something, or take a risk.

Every single person who's ever done something meaningful started scared.

They just didn't let the fear stop them.

So why should you?

There is No "Perfect Time" Coming

You might be telling yourself, "I will start when I feel more confident," or "I will wait till everything falls into place."

But if you are always waiting to feel completely ready... you might be waiting forever.

Life doesn't send an invitation that says, "Now is the perfect time to begin."

You just have to begin-even with the doubt, even with shaky hands, even with fear whispering in your ear.

Progress Happens in the Doing

You don't get better at running by thinking about it-you get better by running.

You don't gain confidence by waiting-you gain it by doing the thing, scared.

Think of Newton's first law: "An object at rest stays at rest." Honestly, that's most of us binge-watching Netflix, waiting for life to magically change. The only way to move forward? Be your own unbalanced force—basically give yourself a loving shove off the couch.

Your first step won't be perfect. Honestly, it might be awkward, messy, even a little painful. But that's part of the process. That's how you learn, and that's how you grow.

And here's the beautiful part: once you take that first step, the next one doesn't feel quite as terrifying. Fear shrinks when you move toward it.

And that's exactly what happened when one young woman finally stopped waiting and started moving.

Bina's First Step

Bina had been dreaming of launching her online art store for over a year. Her sketchbooks were filled, her designs were ready, and yet-she couldn't bring herself to click "publish" on the website she built.

"What if no one buys anything? What if they think it's silly?" she whispered to her best friend one night.

That same friend replied, "So what? At least it's yours."

The next morning, Bina posted her first product with trembling hands and a pit in her stomach. Her first sale didn't come instantly. But when it did, three days later from a stranger, she cried.

Not because she made money. But because she finally started.

That single moment changed everything. She didn't feel ready. She felt terrified.

But she showed up anyway.

Bravery Looks Like Showing Up-Not Having It All Together

We often think brave people feel strong all the time. But they don't.

Brave people feel everything-fear, doubt, insecurity-and they keep going anyway.

You don't need to have it all figured out. You just need to show up.

So maybe today's not about running full speed towards your goal.

Maybe today is just about standing up, taking one shaky breath, and saying,

"I am doing this. Scared or not, I am in."

Because if you are waiting for fear to disappear before you begin...

You will never start.

But if you choose to show up anyway-scared, unsure, messy-you have already done something incredible.

You have started.

Reflection & Journal Page

For Chapter 3: Start Scared, But Start

Be Honest with Yourself

What's one thing you really want to start... but fear keeps holding you back?

(Starting a blog? Speaking up? Applying for something?)

What's the Story in Your Head?

We all have that inner voice that says, "*You can't.*" What's it been telling you lately?

Now flip it. What's a more honest, kind, and helpful story you could tell yourself instead?

Your First (Scary) Step

Big things start small. What's one tiny, brave step you can take this week-even if it scares you?

(It could be making a call, posting a thought, setting a boundary, or just writing the first sentence.)

Your Mantra

Write a sentence you can repeat when fear tries to talk you out of trying.

"Even if I am scared, I will still..."

Chapter 4
Stop Waiting, Start Moving

Because waiting doesn't build anything-movement does.

Let's talk about the waiting game.

You know-the one where you tell yourself:

"I will start once I finish this course."

"I will try when I have more time."

"I just need to figure everything out first."

And just like that, days turn into months. Months into years. And one day you look up and realise... you have been standing still.

Waiting Feels Safe, But It's Not Helping You Grow

It's easy to stay in your head-planning, researching, overthinking. We convince ourselves it's "preparing," but most of the time, it's just a comfortable pause button.

Let me say this with love:

Clarity doesn't always come before action. Sometimes it comes because of it.

The truth? You don't need a perfect plan. You just need to start moving.

Think of it like Newton's First Law—if you're lying on the couch, you'll probably stay there forever... just scrolling reels for the 87th time. The only way to break it? Give yourself a tiny push—because unfortunately, coffee doesn't count as "external force," no matter how strong it is. 😄

Start With What You Have

Maybe you don't have a big following. Maybe you are still figuring out your passion. Maybe you don't feel "qualified."

Guess what?

You are still allowed to begin.

You are allowed to build while you walk. You are allowed to be messy, unsure, and still worthy of chasing what matters to you.

You already have enough to take a first step. You don't need permission from anyone-just a little courage and a lot of honesty.

Movement Builds Confidence-Not the Other Way Around

Most people wait to feel confident before doing something scary. But confidence comes from proof. From trying, from messing up, from seeing, "Hey-I didn't die. I am okay."

The more you move, the more you will trust yourself.

You will stop asking, "Can I really do this?" and start saying, "Wow, I am really doing this."

Bina's Moment of Movement

For weeks, Bina stared at the "Apply Now" button for a creative fellowship she secretly dreamed about. She bookmarked it. Revisited it. Talked herself into it-and out of it-every single day.

One night, frustrated with herself, she opened her laptop and whispered, "Let's just see." Thirty minutes later, her application was submitted. It wasn't perfect. She rewrote her essay three times. Left a typo in her portfolio. But she sent it anyway.

A month later, she got the email: **accepted.**

Not because she was the best. But because she stopped waiting and finally moved.

That one decision opened doors she didn't know existed. Speaking gigs. Clients. Confidence.

All because she clicked a button she was scared of.

Progress Over Perfection

You don't need to sprint. You just need to show up.

Write the first paragraph. Post the first idea. Make the call. Submit the form. Send the email. Walk into the room. Say yes to the thing.

Don't worry if it's not your best. Worry about whether you are staying frozen.

No one builds anything by thinking. They build it by doing.

So, this chapter is your nudge. Maybe even your push.

Stop waiting. Start moving.

Reflection & Journal Page

For Chapter 4: Stop Waiting, Start Moving

What Have You Been Putting Off?

What's that one thing you keep saying you will "start tomorrow"?

(Be honest-you don't have to show this to anyone.)

What Are You Really Waiting For?

Time? Money? Confidence? The "perfect" moment? Write it down. Then ask yourself: is that truly holding you back, or is it an excuse rooted in fear?

Your First Tiny Step

What's *one small thing* you can do today to get the ball rolling? Not a giant leap. Just the first stone.

A Reminder to Come Back To

Write yourself a reminder for when you catch yourself "waiting" again. Make it short, honest, and firm.

"The next step doesn't have to be big; it just has to be..."

Chapter 5: No One is Coming to Save You

It's your life. And it won't change until you decide to take the lead.

This might sound harsh, but it's one of the most freeing truths you will ever hear:

No one is coming.

Not the perfect mentor.

Not the big break.

Not some magical day when everything aligns and the path is suddenly clear.

No one's coming to pull you out of bed, shut down your distractions, and say,

"Now's the time. Let's go."

That responsibility? That power?

It's yours. Always has been.

Honestly, it's like waiting for gravity to suddenly forget how to work–spoiler: it won't. If you want to rise, you'll have to give yourself the lift, because life isn't handing out free helium balloons. hehe

The Hard Truth That Sets You Free

We grow up expecting someone else to give us permission-parents, teachers, bosses, society.

But at some point, you realise: **this is your life.** And no one's going to live it for you.

The longer you wait for someone to show up and fix things, the longer you stay stuck.

You don't need someone to come rescue you.

You need to rescue yourself–with the mindset, choices, and actions that say, **"I am not waiting anymore."**

No One Cares Like You Do-And That's a Good Thing

People might support you. Some might cheer you on.

But no one will ever care about your dream like you do.

They shouldn't. It's yours.

That's not a reason to feel alone. It's a reason to take ownership.

You get to shape your life. You get to say how far you go.

You get to decide what "success" even means to you.

There, is power in that. Real power.

Blame Is Easy. Ownership Is Brave.

It's easy to point fingers-at your past, your circumstances, the people who let you down.

And yes, some of it? It's valid. Life isn't fair. You might have been dealt a harder hand.

But here's what I have learned: **blame doesn't change your life. Ownership does.**

The moment you stop saying "This happened to me," and start saying

"This is where I go from here,"

everything shifts.

Bina's Turning Point

After moving to a new city, Bina thought things would finally fall into place. But weeks turned into months, and nothing "big" happened. Her applications got ignored, her inbox stayed quiet, and her motivation dropped. She spent days waiting, waiting for a mentor to reply, for the "right time," for someone to notice her talent.

One day, she sat on a park bench, completely frustrated. She opened her notes app and typed one sentence:

"No one's coming. So, I am going."

That night, she made a bold choice. She created her own internship-reached out to small businesses offering to redesign their branding for free just to build a portfolio. One said yes. Then another. Then a paying client.

Bina didn't wait for someone to open the door.

She built her own.

No grand gesture. No big break. Just one brave decision to stop waiting and start building.

That's what changed everything.

Lead Yourself First

Waiting for the world to pick you is exhausting.

So instead: **pick yourself.**

Show up for your goals like they matter.

Stick to promises you make to you.

Talk to yourself like someone worth believing in.

Be your own motivation. Your own hype squad. Your own backup plan.

Because when you start leading yourself, the world starts to respond differently.

No one's coming. And that's okay.

You have got what you need. Right now.

Start where you are, lead from within-and rise.

Reflection & Journal Page

For Chapter 5: No One's Coming to Save You

Where Have You Been Waiting for a "Rescue"?

Think of an area in your life where you have been hoping someone or something would change things for you.

Flip the Focus

Now ask yourself: *What is the one thing I can take control of in this situation, starting today?*

Your Self-Leadership Move

What is a decision or an action you can take this week that shows you are showing up for *yourself*?

A Note to Yourself

Write a reminder to come back to when you feel like waiting again. Something short, clear, and powerful.

"I'm not waiting to be chosen. I'm choosing to..."

Chapter 6
Discipline Over Motivation

Because motivation fades, but discipline shows up even when you don't feel like it.

Let's clear something up: motivation is overrated.

It feels good when it hits. You watch a powerful video, hear an inspiring story, or read a quote that fires you up and suddenly you are ready to take on the world.

But the next morning?

You are tired. You don't feel like doing the work. That spark is gone.

And now what?

That's the problem with motivation-it's emotional. It's fleeting. It comes and goes like weather.

Motivation is a Feeling. Discipline is a Choice.

Here's the truth:

The people you look up to? They don't succeed because they are motivated all the time.

They succeed because they have built discipline.

They show up when it is boring.

They keep going when no one is watching.

They do the hard thing even on the days they don't feel like it.

Why?

Because they have decided: **"These matters enough to stay consistent."**

All the motivation in the world won't matter if you don't move.

You Don't Need to Be Inspired to Take Action

We are conditioned to think action follows inspiration.

But often, inspiration comes after action.

You don't wait to feel like brushing your teeth. You just do it. It is a habit.

You can build that same energy into your goals.

Writing. Working out. Studying. Building something.

You do it first. The motivation will catch up.

Think of it like gravity—you can't see it, but it's always pulling you down to sit on the couch. Discipline is basically you deciding to be the rocket that fights gravity… even if your "fuel" is just one cup of coffee and pure stubbornness. hehe

Discipline is Just Keeping a Promise to Yourself

And honestly? That's where most of us struggle, not with effort, but with self-trust.

Every time you show up when it's hard, you send yourself a message:

"I can count on me."

And that changes everything.

Discipline doesn't have to mean extreme routines or military-level willpower.

It just means you don't abandon yourself every time the excitement wears off.

Start Small. Keep Showing Up.

The secret is consistency. Not intensity.

Don't aim to do everything at once. Aim to do something every day-no matter how small.

10 minutes of writing. 5 pages of reading. 15 minutes of movement.

Tiny things that add up. That's discipline. That's progress.

And when others stop because they don't "feel like it," you will still be moving.

Quietly. Steadily. Powerfully.

Bina's 15-Minute Rule

There was a point when Bina almost gave up on creating content. Her job was exhausting, her audience was small, and most days she didn't "feel creative."

So, she made herself a deal: **15 minutes a day, no matter what.**

Write a post. Sketch a concept. Share an idea. Even if it sucked. Even if no one saw it.

Some days, that 15 minutes turned into an hour. Some days, it didn't. But she showed up. And slowly, her consistency started doing what motivation couldn't-**build real momentum.**

A year later, that tiny daily habit became her full-time career.

Not because she always felt inspired. But because she kept a promise—to herself.

Some days, the spark won't light—

you will scroll, you will sigh,

you will swear tomorrow feels more right.

But habits don't wait for moods to bloom,

they show up in a quiet room,

where no one claps,

and nothing's new,

just you-

and the work you said you'd do.

Motivation flares, then fades like mist,

but discipline?

That's the steady fist

that knocks each day,

rain or shine,

and says,

"It's time. The rest is mine."

Motivation feels good, but discipline gets things done.

So on the days you are not feeling it-**remember why you started.**

Then get up, show up, and do the thing anyway.

Reflection & Journal Page

For Chapter 6: Discipline Over Motivation

What Have You Been Relying on Motivation For?

Be honest-what's one goal you keep putting off unless you are "in the mood"?

Flip the Script

What's one small action you can commit to daily-even when motivation is missing?

→ I will do this consistently, even when I don't feel like it:

Build Self-Trust

Write a short message to remind yourself why showing up matters-especially when it is hard.

"Every time I show up for myself, I prove that..."

Your Simple Daily Habit (No Excuses)

Pick one non-negotiable habit you will do for the next 7 days—no matter what.

→ My one thing:

Chapter 7
Cut the Noise

Because not everything deserves your attention–and not everyone gets a seat at your table.

The world is loud.

It's shouting at you every minute:

"Be more. Do more. Look like this. Think like that."

Notifications. Opinions. Comparisons. Expectations.

And in the middle of all that noise... it's hard to hear yourself.

Let's be real: how many times have you started doubting your own path-not because it didn't feel right, but because it didn't look like someone else's highlight reel?

That's the danger of noise.

It pulls you away from your own voice.

Not All Noise is Negative–But It is Still Distracting

Sometimes the noise is obvious: endless scrolling, toxic people, mindless routines.

But sometimes it is sneaky-like constantly seeking approval, overcommitting to please others, or listening to too many voices at once.

It all adds up. And slowly, it blurs your direction.

If you are feeling overwhelmed, scattered, unsure-it is probably not because you don't know what you want. It is because you can't hear it anymore.

Your Energy is Not Unlimited—Spend it Wisely

You don't need to respond to every message.

You don't need to jump on every trend.

You don't need to explain yourself to people who are not trying to understand.

Protect your energy like it's something valuable-because it is.

When you cut the noise, you make space for clarity. Focus. Peace.

And that's where real progress begins.

Think of it like signal and noise in physics—if your "life signal" is too weak, all the outside noise drowns it out. And trust me, you don't want to live like a bad radio station stuck between two channels.

Say No Without Apologizing

One of the bravest things you can do is say:

"This doesn't serve me right now."

That could mean:

- Saying no to plans that leave you drained
- Logging off social media for a while
- Setting boundaries with people who constantly distract or discourage you
- Choosing quiet over constant input

It doesn't mean you are rude. It is a sign you are choosing yourself.

Bina's Moment of Quiet

For weeks, Bina had been feeling lost. She was working hard, doing "everything right," and still felt stuck. Her phone buzzed non-stop—group chats, content deadlines, trending challenges, constant comparisons. Every time she scrolled, she felt further from herself.

One evening, after an especially exhausting day, she turned off her phone and went for a walk—no music, no podcast, just silence. It felt strange at first. But by the time she returned, something had shifted.

She didn't have all the answers. But she knew one thing for sure: **she couldn't keep living at the volume of everyone else's voice.**

The next day, she set new boundaries. Deleted the apps that drained her. Said no without guilt. She didn't disappear; she just stopped letting the noise decide her next move.

And slowly, her mind got quieter. Her decisions got clearer. And she started building againnot louder, but deeper.

Silence Isn't Emptiness—It is Power

You don't need constant stimulation to feel alive.

Some of your biggest ideas, breakthroughs, and shifts will come in moments of stillness.

So, step back. Breathe. Turn down the volume.

Ask yourself: **"What really matters right now?"**

Because when you cut the noise, you can finally hear the most important voice of all-**your own.**

When the noise dies down and the lists are done,

and you are left alone with the setting sun-

breathe, and listen-soft but clear-

that voice inside is what got you here.

Reflection & Journal Page

For Chapter 7: Cut the Noise

What has Been Distracting You Lately?

Social media? Negative people? Constant comparison? Be honest, what's pulling you away from your focus?

What Are You Ready to Let Go Of?

Choose one thing you will reduce, mute, or remove this week to clear your mind and refocus.

→ I am ready to limit or step away from:

Create a Boundary That Protects Your Energy

Write one sentence that feels like a personal boundary you are going to start honoring.

"I give myself permission to say no to..."

Make Space for Quiet

Even 5 minutes of stillness can shift your mindset. How will you build quiet time into your day?

→ My quiet time looks like:

Chapter 8
Listen to Your Own Voice

Because the answers you seek aren't out there-they are already within you.

Once you cut the noise, something powerful happens.

At first, it feels uncomfortable-like stepping out of a crowded room and into silence.

Your brain still buzzes. You reach for your phone out of habit. You wonder, *What now?*

But then... a stillness settles.

And in that stillness, you start to hear it—

your own voice.

Not the one shaped by opinions, expectations, or likes.

The real one. The one you hid beneath all the "musts" and "have to's."

It's quieter than the noise-but clearer.

And it knows what you really want.

Think of it like quantum physics—where particles don't "decide" what they are until you actually observe

them. Your life feels the same way: if you keep looking at everyone else's path, your own possibilities just sit there in a superposition of meh. 😄 *The moment you focus inward? Boom—you collapse the wave function and actually choose a reality.*

You Already Know

Here's the truth no one says loud enough:

You are not as lost as you think.

You already know what lights you up.

You already feel when something is off.

You already sense when you are settling.

But when you are constantly surrounded by noise-comparison, pressure, outside validation-you stop trusting that voice.

You overthink. You second-guess. You outsource your intuition.

You let someone else's path become your map.

But your voice? It is still there. Waiting.

Not to shout, but to guide.

"Bina's story unfolded in silence, in the spaces where strength often goes unnoticed. But Ayaan's shift came

differently, through restlessness, doubt, and a moment that finally made him pause and ask, 'Is this really the life I want?'"

From Confusion to Clarity: Ayaan's Turning Point

Ayaan had always been a deep thinker-the kind who got stuck in endless research, advice columns, and expert podcasts, always searching for the "right" way to move forward.

After his first nervous open mic performance, something shifted. He showed up. He was seen. And it didn't break him. In fact, it gave him something he hadn't felt in a long time: momentum.

But soon, the noise returned.

Well-meaning friends told him to play it safe. Family encouraged more "secure" paths. His social media was full of people who looked like they had it all figured out.

Before long, his mind felt louder than ever. That small spark he'd found? It started to fade.

One weekend, he took a train ride with no real destination. He left his phone in his backpack and just stared out the window. He journaled. Watched people. Breathed.

For the first time in months, he wasn't trying to chase anything or prove anything. He was just being present. Just listening.

And somewhere between two quiet stations, a question came to him:

"What would I do if no one was watching?"

He wrote it down.

And in shaky handwriting, he answered:

"I'd build things that help people. I'd speak. I'd write."

That was the start of real clarity.

Not because a coach told him to. Not because a motivational reel said so.

But because he finally got quite enough to hear his own voice.

Give Yourself Permission to Decide

No one else has to "get it" for it to be real.

You don't need to justify your dream.

You don't need everyone's blessing.

You just need *you*-your clarity, your reasons, your next right step.

Ask yourself:

- "What am I doing because I *want* to-and what am I doing because I *think I should*?"
- "Where am I muting myself just to keep peace?"

- "What truth have I been too afraid to say out loud?"

And then: say it. Write it. Follow it.

Even if it is small.

Even if it is scary.

Even if it is different from what everyone else is doing.

Your Voice Deserves Space

You don't discover your voice by waiting for approval.

You find it by choosing to speak-even when your words shake.

Especially when they shake.

Write that post. Say what's on your heart. Begin what's been calling you.

It might not come out perfectly-but it will be *authentically* yours.

And that's what truly counts.

Because every time you use your voice, it grows-not in volume, but in truth.

From Listening to Leading

When Ayaan started trusting his own voice, something else happened.

He stopped obsessing over likes and started focusing on impact.

He shared lessons from his journey online-not polished tips, but honest reflections.

And slowly, people started showing up.

First, a few classmates. Then, students from other colleges.

They resonated with his honesty. His imperfect progress. His voice.

What started as a whisper became a movement.

Not because he was the best.

But because he was *real.*

Let This Be Your Invitation

Silence the noise.

Listen inward.

Then let that voice guide you.

Not because it guarantees a straight path—but because it guarantees *your* path.

You don't need to have it all figured out.

You just need to *start* trusting the voice that's been there all along.

Reflection Journal

For Chapter 8: Listen to Your Own Voice

1. What messages or "noise" have been influencing your decisions lately?

Be honest. Are they helping-or holding you back?

2. When was the last time you felt deeply connected to your own intuition?

What were you doing? Who were you with? How can you create more of that?

3. Write your inner truth:

"What do I truly want right now, even if it doesn't make sense to others?"

4. Write one decision you will make this week—just for you.

→ I will: ___________________________

Chapter 9
Build Your Own Path

Because you weren't born to fit into someone else's idea of success.

It is easy to fall into the trap of following someone else's roadmap.

We see what others are doing-friends, influencers, society-and without even realising it, we start measuring our lives against theirs.

We choose jobs we don't love.

We chase degrees we are not passionate about.

We Walk paths we were never meant to be on-all because they are "*safe,*" "*approved,*" or "*expected.*"

But here's something no one says loud enough:

It is okay to want something different.

Your journey won't look like theirs-

and that is okay.

You might take detours,

hit pause,

start late,

or change your mind halfway.

But every step is still progress.

Every stumble still counts.

You are not behind-

you are just on *your* way.

Your Journey Doesn't Have to Look Like Theirs

Maybe your path doesn't come with titles, promotions, or applause.

Maybe it's unconventional, messy, or slower than others. That doesn't make it wrong.

In fact, it probably means you are being honest with yourself.

And honesty is rare. It's also powerful.

The people who truly build something meaningful in life?

They stop copying-and start creating.

They grew tired of copying every trend,

chasing paths that never truly blend.

One quiet day, they took the chance-

to build their life, not just glance.

It's a bit like electrons—everyone assumes they'll just follow the same orbit because "that's what electrons do," but then one jumps to a higher energy level and surprises everyone. That could be you—choosing the jump no one expects, even if it makes other people uncomfortable.

It Takes Courage to Walk a Road Few Understand

When you decide to carve your own path, not everyone will get it.

You will face questions, doubts, maybe even silence.

"Why would you leave that job?"

"Are you sure this is the right move?"

"That sounds risky."

It's uncomfortable. But it's worth it.

Because at the end of the day, you are the one who has to live with your choices—not the people commenting on them.

From Questions to Creation: Elena's Leap of Faith

Ayaan's turning point came through restlessness and doubt.

Elena's began with a quiet pull-one she couldn't ignore, even as everything around her followed a predictable path.

Elena was in her final year of college, preparing for campus placements. Most of her friends had already landed job offers in IT companies or were applying to management programs. She followed suit-not because she loved it, but because it felt like the "next logical step."

But in the quiet hours between lectures and late-night dorm conversations, Elena couldn't shake the feeling that something was missing. She had always loved visual storytelling-designing posters for college events, editing videos, playing with typography. It had been a hobby, never a "career option."

Still, the pull was strong. Elena started taking up small freelance gigs-logos for local cafés, digital invites for weddings, Instagram creatives for startups. What started as weekend work became a full-blown obsession.

When she told her parents she didn't want to sit for placements, they were stunned.

"You are wasting your degree," her father said.

"Designing graphics isn't a job-it's a side thing," her uncle chimed in.

It took time. And uncomfortable conversations. Elena agreed to freelance while interning part-time at a design agency to show she was serious. Slowly, her work started speaking for itself.

Today, Elena is building a career that feels real. Not perfect, not viral-*real.*

Some months are better than others. She is learning about clients, feedback, invoices, and burnout. But for the first time, she wakes up excited to create.

She may not have a corporate title.

But she has clarity.

She has courage.

And she's finally living a life that looks like hers-not a borrowed version of someone else's.

She stopped chasing what made others proud,

stepped out from the safe, familiar crowd.

Now her days are stitched with fire and grace-

each moment shaped in her own bold pace.

It is not perfect, not always neat,

but her heart beats strong in every beat.

Comparison is a Thief. Purpose is a Compass.

You will never feel-good chasing someone else's dream.

And here's the thing: your version of success might not look impressive to everyone.

But if it makes you feel alive, grounded, fulfilled-that's more than enough.

So, stop measuring your life with someone else's ruler.

Start asking: **"What actually matters to me?"**

And then start building from there.

There is No "Right" Way-Only Your Way

There is no single path to a meaningful life.

You don't need to follow trends or check every box.

You just need to listen to your own voice-and trust that it's enough to guide you.

Build a path that makes sense to you. Even if no one else gets it *yet*.

Because someday, someone else will look at your journey and think:

"If they can do it their way, I can too."

Reflection Journal: Chapter 9– Build Your Own Path

Take a quiet moment. Answer these questions honestly-there's no right or wrong.

What lights me up-even if I have been calling it "just a hobby"?

If no one judged my decisions, what would I choose to do differently right now?

What is the one small step I can take this week to explore my own path?

What fears are holding me back from taking that step-and how can I face them gently?

What would "success" feel like-not look like-for me?

Whose Expectations Are You Carrying?

Think about any pressure you have felt to live a certain way. Is it coming from you-or someone else?

What Does *Your* Path Look Like?

If no one was watching or judging, what would you *actually* want to do, learn, build, or become?

One Step Away from Comparison

What is the one habit or trigger that leads you to compare yourself to others-and how can you reduce it?

→ **I will stop comparing myself by:**

A Reminder to Stay Grounded

Write a personal truth or statement to help you keep walking your own path when doubt creeps in.

"My life doesn't need to look like anyone else's, because..."

Chapter 10
Lead from Where You Are

Because leadership isn't about being the loudest-it's about showing up, even when you are unsure.

Leadership isn't the tallest shout,

it is standing firm when filled with doubt.

It's quiet strength, a steady light,

that guides the way through darkest night.

When you think of the word "leader," what comes to mind?

Maybe someone in a suit commanding a room.

Or a social media influencer with thousands of followers.

Or the head of a team giving powerful speeches.

But real leadership? It often looks quieter than that.

It's someone who dares to go first-

Even when they don't have a title.

Even when no one's clapping yet.

Even when the path is still forming beneath their feet.

It is the student who speaks up in a class where no one else will.

It is the artist who shares a rough draft and says, "These matters to me."

It is *you*-right now-deciding to live honestly and bravely.

You don't need a platform to make an impact.

You don't need permission to lead.

You just need to start showing up as the real you.

Ayaan's First "Yes"

After Ayaan's pitch night and his train ride of clarity, he began showing up a little differently.

He didn't overhaul his life overnight. He didn't quit college or build a million-dollar startup in a month.

But he made one quiet promise to himself:

To stop hiding.

To start being seen in motion-not just in potential.

He created a Telegram group called **"Build in Public: Student Edition."** No fancy logo. Just a space for sharing small wins, big questions, and honest updates.

At first, only 6 people joined-friends and classmates.

But Ayaan treated those 6 like they mattered.

Every week, he posted:

"What did you learn this week that others might need to hear?"

"What are you building-even if it's messy?"

"Where are you stuck-and what's one tiny step you can take?"

People started replying. Then inviting others.

What started as a whisper... began to grow.

What Makes a Leader?

Not a title.

Not a perfect resume.

Not having it all figured out.

A leader is someone who dares to say:

"I will go first-even if I fail."

"I will speak up-even if my voice shakes."

"I will lift others as I rise."

And here's the best part: when you show up as yourself, *you give other people permission to do the same.*

That's exactly what Ayaan did-without shouting, selling, or performing.

Just by being consistent. Honest. Brave enough to try.

But What If I am Not Ready?

Here's the truth: no one ever *feels* ready.

Every creator, speaker, founder, artist, or dreamer you admire?

They all started from zero.

They all had a moment where they wanted to turn around.

Where they thought, *who am I to lead?*

But the real question is: *Who are you not to?*

You have something only you can give.

An idea. A perspective. A way of connecting.

And someone, somewhere, needs exactly that-delivered in your voice, your tone, your way.

Small Steps, Big Ripples

Leadership doesn't always look dramatic.

Sometimes it is:

Replying to someone else's question with kindness.

Starting a weekly reflection journal and inviting others to join.

Recording your first podcast episode on your phone with no fancy mic-just heart.

Ayaan didn't know what his group would become.

But a year later, that tiny Telegram group had turned into a campus-wide event series.

Young creators shared their work. Tech students taught design. Designers helped engineers tell better stories.

It wasn't a company.

It was community.

All because one person stopped waiting-and started showing up.

You Lead by Being You

You don't have to shout.

You don't have to go viral.

You don't have to chase anyone else's blueprint.

The most powerful thing you can do is lead from *right where you are.*

With your own voice. Your own pace. Your own why.

And when you do?

You not only rise-you *lift.*

Reflection Journal

For Chapter 10: Lead from Where You Are

1. **What's one space in your life where you have been waiting for someone else to go first?**
2. What would it look like if *you* led the way?
3. **Who is someone who inspires you by how they lead quietly, honestly, or consistently?**
4. What can you learn from them?
5. **What can you start, share, or support this week—even if it's small or imperfect?**
6. One small leadership move I will make: ____________________
7. **Write your own leadership mantra.**
8. "I lead by..." ____________________

Chapter 11
You Will Fail — Good

Because failure is not the opposite of progress-it is a part of it.

By now, you have met Bina-the one who stepped off the beaten path to build something of her own.

But here's the thing no one really prepares you for:

When you choose courage over comfort, failure often shows up first.

That's exactly what happened to Aarav.

Let's just say it straight:

You are going to fail.

Probably more than once.

Probably in ways that sting.

Maybe even in public.

And honestly?

That is good.

It means you are trying.

It means you are moving.

It means you are brave enough to do something that could go wrong-and that is how all great things begin.

Failure Isn't Final-It's Feedback

When we are young, failure feels like the end. A red mark. A closed door.

But real growth? It usually starts *after* things fall apart.

Because failure teaches in ways success never could:

- It shows you where you need to grow.
- It teaches you how to adapt.
- It builds resilience–something you'll never learn while playing it safe.

You don't lose when you fail.

You lose when you quit.

You are Allowed to Fall Apart before you rise

It is okay to cry.

It is okay to feel embarrassed.

It is okay to want to give up for a minute.

Just don't unpack and live there.

Let yourself feel it-and then ask,

"What is this trying to teach me?"

Because once you see failure as a teacher, it loses its power to shame you.

Failure knocked, and yes-it stung,

left my pride a little undone.

But when I looked it in the eye,

it didn't laugh-it asked me *why?*

So, I sat, and learned, and tried again,

less afraid of falling than I'd been.

Turns out, mistakes don't end the race—

they teach you how to find your pace.

Aarav's Broken Pitch

Aarav had been working on his startup idea for almost a year. It was bold-an app designed to connect rural artisans directly with urban buyers. Everyone he shared it with said it was "innovative," "impactful," "needed."

He finally got a chance to pitch it at a youth entrepreneurship summit. A big platform. High hopes.

And then, everything fell apart.

His presentation glitched. He forgot his key talking points. The judges asked questions he hadn't prepared for. His voice shook. He walked off the stage feeling humiliated.

That night, he told himself he was done.

But the next day, one of the organizers reached out. "Your idea is solid," she said. "You just need to prepare better. I can mentor you, if you are willing to keep going."

Aarav didn't get the funding that day.

But he got something better: clarity, direction, and a reason to keep building.

Six months later, his reworked pitch won a grant. His platform is now live in three states, and growing.

What felt like failure was really the **first draft** of something real.

No One Gets Good Without Failing First

Want to be great at anything?

Prepare to be bad at it first.

No one posts their failed drafts, messy rehearsals, or awkward first tries. But they are there-behind every success story is a graveyard of failed attempts.

Think of it like learning physics—everyone bombs their first attempt at understanding quantum mechanics. But just like Schrödinger's cat, your

success is both alive and dead until you keep trying. The only way to "open the box" is to actually do the work (and fail a few times) first

So, stop expecting perfection on your first go.

Start expecting progress.

Start celebrating trying.

You are Not Behind. You are Becoming.

Some people will rise faster.

Some will "win" sooner. That is fine.

Don't let someone else's timeline trick you into thinking you are not moving.

Every setback you face is part of your story.

Not the end of it.

So, when you fall?

Fall forward.

Take the lesson.

Stand up.

Move again.

Because failure doesn't mean the rise is over.

It just means it is getting real.

Reflection Journal: Chapter 11 – You Will Fail – Good

What Stuck with Me

"Failure isn't the opposite of progress-it's part of it."

This chapter helped me shift how I see failure-from something to avoid, to something I can learn from. Aarav's story reminded me that even when things fall apart, they can still be the start of something meaningful.

1. Recall a Failure

Think of a time when something didn't go the way you planned. Write about what happened.

- What did it feel like at the time?
- What story did you tell yourself afterward?

My thoughts:

2. What Did It Teach You?

Looking back-was there anything that situation taught you?

- Did it point out a gap in your skills?
- Did it reveal what truly matters to you?

What I learned:

3. How Did You Respond?

Be honest: Did you give up? Hide? Try again?

- What would you do differently today?

My response was:

Next time, I will:

4. Letting Go of Shame

The chapter says: “Once you see failure as a teacher, it loses its power to shame you.”

- What failures are you still holding shame over?
- What would it feel like to release that shame?

I still carry shame around...

...

But maybe it’s time to see it as...

5. Your "Fall Forward" Plan

What’s something you’ve been avoiding because you’re scared to fail?

- What's one small, brave step you can take this week to move forward anyway?

I have been avoiding...

...

One step I can take is...

Key Takeaways

- Failure means I am *in motion*, not broken.
- I don't have to get it perfect-I just have to *keep going.*
- Setbacks don't mean I am behind. I am becoming.

Quote to Keep Close

"You don't lose when you fail. You lose when you quit."

Chapter 12
Stay in the Game

Because the ones who win are usually the ones who don't walk away.

You are going to have days when it feels like nothing is working.

You are trying. You are showing up. You are doing the hard things.

And still-it's quiet. No breakthrough. No big win.

No sign that you are even on the right track.

That's when most people stop.

They say, "Maybe I am not cut out for this."

They quit three feet from the gold.

But this chapter is your reminder:

Don't leave the game just because it is taking time.

Progress Is Quiet Before It is Loud

You won't always see the results of your effort right away.

Sometimes, the seeds you planted are growing underground,

doing the slow, invisible work of becoming something real.

Your job isn't to rush the outcome.

Your job is to keep showing up.

Keep showing up when it is boring.

Keep showing up when it is slow.

Keep showing up when you are the only one clapping for yourself.

That's how momentum is built.

That's how people rise.

Think of it like trying to boil water—at 99°C, nothing happens, and you're staring at the pot like "Why am I even doing this?"... but one more degree and boom—it's steam, baby! Physics reminds us: results don't show until you keep adding heat... so don't turn off the stove just yet.

Aarav's Slow Climb

After his first failed pitch, Aarav almost gave up on his startup idea.

But something in him said, "*You're not done yet.*"

So he got back to work.

For months, he operated out of a tiny room in his parents' house,

cold-calling artisans, redesigning his app, and pitching to anyone who would listen.

Most days were silent. No applause. No validation.

He worked full-time and freelanced on weekends just to keep the idea alive.

There were delays. Rejections. Moments where it all felt pointless.

But he kept showing up. Even on the days that felt empty.

Eventually, a small grant came through. Then a local NGO offered to collaborate.

Today, Aarav's platform is helping hundreds of rural artisans sell their craft in cities they have never even visited.

It didn't happen fast.

It didn't happen with noise.

It happened because he **stayed in the game.**

It took long nights and quiet tries,

moments no one glorifies.

No spotlight, cheer, or perfect plan-
just showing up, again and again.
The wins came slow, the doubt ran deep,
but he held on when others' sleep.
Not magic, luck, or instant fame-
just grit that kept him in the game.

Persistence Is More Powerful Than Talent

Some people will have more advantages. More skills. More support.

But persistence? That's the equalizer.

You don't need to be the fastest, smartest, or most talented.

You just need to **outlast your doubts.**

Keep learning. Keep growing. Keep going.

Because the ones who rise aren't always the most gifted-

they are the ones who **refuse to give up.**

Fall Behind? Get Back In.

You are going to fall off track. That's life. It is not a reason to quit.

You don't need a perfect record-you need the ability to **restart.**

Whether it is a day, a week, or even a year-

you can always re-enter the game.

Every time you come back, you come back stronger.

You Don't Need Motivation-You Need Memory

On the hard days, don't ask yourself how you feel.

Ask yourself:

- *Why did I begin?*
- *Who am I becoming?*
- *What happens if I keep going?*

Remembering your *why* helps you keep moving-long after the motivation fades.

So, breathe. Reset. Get back in the game.

Because the only real failure is walking away

when your future is still waiting.

Reflection Journal: Chapter 12 – Stay in the Game

This chapter is about perseverance, especially when things feel slow, uncertain, or invisible. Use the space below to reconnect with your journey, your "why," and your strength to keep going.

1. What goal or dream am I working toward right now that feels like it's taking longer than I expected?

Describe where you are and what you are feeling about it.

2. What does "progress" look like for me today-even if it is not loud or visible yet?

Write down any small wins you have had recently (even if no one else saw them).

3. Have I ever given up on something too soon?

What might have changed if I'd stayed in the game a little longer?

4. When was the last time I showed up, even when I didn't feel like it?

How did it feel afterward? What did I learn from that moment?

5. Aarav didn't win immediately-but he kept showing up. What's one way I can show up this week, even if no one's watching or clapping?

Be specific: a task, a habit, a step.

6. What's my "why"?

Write down your core reason for starting this journey. What's driving you to stay in the game-even when it's hard?

"I don't have to feel ready. I just have to keep showing up."

– Your Future Self

Chapter 13
Start Again - Stronger

Because coming back is a superpower, too.

You stayed in the game.

You gave it your time, your energy, your heart.

But sometimes, even with all that effort, things still fall apart.

And when they do?

You will hear that quiet voice in your head whisper:

"Maybe I wasn't good enough. Maybe I shouldn't try again."

But what if this isn't the end?

What if this is just your restart?

Starting Over Isn't a Step Back

Taking a break doesn't mean giving up.

Pausing doesn't mean you have failed.

Sometimes, you need to let the old version go-to come back stronger, clearer, and wiser.

Because starting again doesn't make you weak.

It means you are brave enough to rebuild from the truth.

Think of it like potential energy—you might be at the bottom of the hill now, but you're just storing up power for the next climb. Gravity may pull you down, but hey, what goes down can always climb back up... especially if you've got snacks for the hike.

Sabrina's Second Launch

Sabrina had always been passionate about food-especially traditional recipes passed down by her grandmother.

So, after years of working a desk job she didn't love, she took a bold step: she opened a cloud kitchen serving regional comfort food with a modern twist.

It started well-local buzz, some media features, steady orders.

But logistics were tough. Her delivery app partnerships fell through. Rising costs ate into her margins. She stretched herself thin doing everything-from cooking to packaging to customer support.

By the end of year one, Sabrina was exhausted.

A few bad reviews hit her confidence hard. Orders slowed. Her small team left for more stable work.

Eventually, she shut it down. Quietly. With guilt.

For a while, she didn't touch a stove.

But the love never left her.

One day, while helping at a friend's housewarming, someone asked, *"Did you ever think of teaching cooking?"*

That question stuck.

Within weeks, she began filming simple recipe videos from her phone. No fancy setup-just her kitchen, her voice, her story.

Soon, her videos picked up. People resonated with the warmth and honesty. She started hosting virtual cooking classes, then small in-person workshops.

Today, Sabrina doesn't run a kitchen-she runs a food community.

She's not chasing scale. She's building depth.

And it's working-on *her* terms.

She didn't make it because she never failed.

She made it because she didn't let failure have the final say.

It's Okay to Change the Plan-Not the Dream

You might not restart from the same point.

But you restart with experience.

That's what gives your next chapter more depth, more strength, more soul.

It is not about bouncing back.

It is about building forward-with intention.

Progress Isn't Always a Straight Line

Sometimes, moving ahead means:

- Taking a step sideways.
- Letting go of what burned you out.
- Trusting a quieter path.

Success isn't about never falling.

It is about what you do *after* your fall.

Your Comeback Will Carry Wisdom

Sabrina didn't "go viral."

She didn't get lucky.

She simply asked herself:

What's still possible, even now?

So, if you are tired, unsure, or starting over-take heart.

You haven't failed. You have learned.

And now? You begin again. Better equipped. More honest. More *you*.

Let This Be Your Reminder:

- Begin again, even if your hands are still shaking.
- Start from scratch if you must.
- Choose peace over pressure.

- But *don't stay stuck.*

Because your restart might be the most powerful move you ever make.

You thought it ended-

the dream, the fight,

but here you are,

still holding light.

It's not too late,

you're not too far-

a restart isn't weakness,

it's knowing who you are.

Begin again,

even if it's slow-

sometimes the best things

are the ones that grow.

Reflection Journal: Chapter 13 – Start Again, Stronger

"Your restart might be the most powerful move you ever make."

Pause & Reflect

Take a breath. This space is for you to be honest-with yourself, for yourself.

1. When Have You Started Over?

Think of a time when something you tried didn't work out.

- What happened?
- What made you stop-or pause?

My story:

2. What Did You Learn from That Experience?

Every ending carries a message. What did that chapter teach you-about yourself, your limits, or your strengths?

Lessons I found in the mess:

3. Let Go of the Guilt

Bina's story reminds us that closing something down doesn't mean you failed—it means you were willing to try.

- What part of your past do you still feel guilty or ashamed about?
- What would it look like to forgive yourself?

I am ready to release...

4. What's Still Possible Now?

Even if the original dream changed, your purpose is still here.

- What do you *still* want to build, do, or become?

Right now, I still believe in...

5. Create Your Restart Plan

This isn't about reinventing everything overnight.

- What's *one small step* you can take to begin again?
- Who can you ask for help, support, or encouragement?

My next small move:

...

Someone I can reach out to:

Grounding Reminder

"It's not about bouncing back. It's about building forward-with intention."

You are not behind. You are not broken.

You are becoming. In your own time, in your own way.

Chapter 14
Grow Through What You Go Through

Because real progress often happens in the places no one claps for.

By now, you know this:

Your path won't always look like progress.

There will be seasons where everything feels still. Where effort outweighs results. Where it feels like everyone else is moving ahead-and you are just… stuck.

But here's what's often overlooked:

Growth is not always visible.

And progress doesn't always come with recognition.

Sometimes, you grow the most when you're just trying to hold it together.

Growth Isn't a Straight Line

We think growth looks like:

- A better title
- A bigger team
- A corner office

But real growth?

It looks like:

- Saying no when it's easier to say yes
- Asking for help when your pride says don't
- Choosing calm in the middle of chaos

It is the stuff you *can't* put on your resume-but it is what shapes your future more than anything else.

Think of it like potential energy in physics—you might feel like you're just a rock sitting at the top of a hill. No movement, no applause. But the moment the right push comes along—boom—you're in motion, and suddenly you're kinetic. Unless friction (aka Netflix or the snooze button) tries to stop you. Haha

Also, don't worry if your progress graph looks more like a badly drawn sine wave. Physics taught us: oscillations are normal. What matters is—you're still vibrating with purpose.

Rohan's Shift

Rohan had always been an overachiever. He joined his dream firm right after business school, aiming to climb fast. Promotions, presentations, client wins-he checked every box.

But three years in, something shifted. He was leading a team for the first time-and it wasn't going well.

His confidence cracked under pressure. His team seemed disengaged. His emails went unanswered. He didn't know how to delegate without micromanaging, or how to connect without feeling awkward.

For the first time, Rohan wasn't the rising star. He was just... stuck.

He thought about switching jobs. About starting over somewhere new.

But something told him to stay.

Not out of fear-but because deep down, he knew: **this was the part he needed to grow through.**

So, he got quiet. He started asking for feedback-real, uncomfortable feedback.

He sat with his mistakes.

He learned how to listen instead of lead with ego.

He started one-on-ones with his team-not to give instructions, but to understand them.

Slowly, the dynamic changed. Trust returned. Results improved. Not overnight-but over time.

Rohan didn't get an award for that season.

But what he gained was deeper:

Clarity. Patience. Emotional range.

Today, he still works at the same company.

He hasn't jumped to a flashier role.

But the people who work with him say this:

"Rohan is someone you grow under. Someone who's done the work to become steady."

Progress That Doesn't Post Well

In a world obsessed with outcomes, don't underestimate the power of internal progress:

- The courage to speak in the meeting you used to hide in.
- The restraint to *not* react.
- The humility to start again, without needing applause.

That is not falling behind.

That is becoming who you are meant to be.

Grow Now, Shine Later

Some seasons are for building.

Some are for blooming.

And if you are in a quiet season?

Let it build you.

You are not late.

You are not less.

You are just learning lessons that last longer than titles ever do.

Let This Be Your Reminder:

- Growth doesn't always look like winning.
- Progress doesn't always look like more.
- You are allowed to evolve at your own pace-without needing to prove it to anyone.

You don't have to be the loudest in the room.

Just be the one who keeps growing when no one's watching.

Because that's the kind of growth that changes everything.

It didn't look like winning,

no spotlight, no applause-

just quiet steps on tired days,

still showing up because.

No big reveal, no perfect plan,

just lessons learned along the way-

and that slow, invisible kind of growth

that's changing you each day.

Reflection Journal: Chapter 14 – Grow Through What You Go Through

"You're not behind. You're becoming."

1. Acknowledge the Unseen Work

Not all progress is loud.

Think about the ways you have grown recently-even if no one noticed.

In what areas of your life or work have you grown quietly?

(e.g., handling pressure, being more assertive, setting boundaries)

I have grown in...

2. Reflect on a "Stuck" Season

We all go through seasons that feel like nothing's moving.

But often, those are the seasons that shape us most.

Was there a time at work (or in life) when you felt stuck-but ended up learning something important?

- What did you learn?
- How did it change you?

Looking back, I see that season taught me...

3. Redefine What Progress Looks Like

Forget titles and milestones for a second.

Let's get personal.

What does *progress* mean to you right now?

Not what the world expects-what *you* need.

For me, progress means...

4. Honor Your Effort

Maybe no one clapped.

Maybe no one even noticed.

But you kept showing up-and that matters.

What's something you have done recently that you are proud of-even if it wasn't perfect or praised?

I am proud that I...

5. Set an Intention for Your Growth

Growth doesn't have to be big to be meaningful.

Set a gentle goal for yourself.

What's one way you want to keep growing in the next few weeks or months?

I want to grow in...

And I will do that by...

...

Gentle Reminder

"You don't have to shine every season.

But if you're growing-

even slowly-

you are already on your way."

Chapter 15
When They Try to Define Your Limits

Because just because they can't see your potential doesn't mean it's not there.

Let's be honest-

Sometimes you do everything right.

You meet deadlines. You lead quietly. You support your team.

And still, someone else gets the praise. The spotlight. The promotion.

And you're left wondering,

What more do I need to do?

That moment-when your effort gets overlooked,

when someone tells you to "wait your turn,"

or suggests you are not "quite ready yet"?

Those stings.

And it can start to make you doubt what you once knew for sure:

That you are capable.

That you have earned it.

That you deserve to grow.

Think of it like dark matter in physics—just because people can't "see" it, doesn't mean it isn't holding the whole galaxy together. Your impact might be invisible to some, but it's still shaping everything around you... silently flexing those gravitational vibes. Hehe

It's Not Always About You—But It Still Hurts

Sometimes it's politics.

Sometimes it's bias.

Sometimes it's just a broken system that rewards noise over nuance.

Whatever it is—

You feel it.

The invisible wall.

The way they celebrate potential in others, but ask you to "prove it" ten times over.

And while the world says, "Don't take it personally,"

how can you not?

It is personal.

You are trying. And it feels like it is still not enough.

Tanvi's Story: Seen Too Late

Tanvi had always been the steady one on the team.

The one who stayed back when a deadline went sideways.

The one who fixed the errors quietly.

The one who made space for others to shine.

But when leadership roles came up?

They picked louder voices.

People who were good at talking, even if they weren't great at doing.

Her manager said,

"You are brilliant... but maybe you need to be a bit more visible."

At first, Tanvi took it to heart.

Maybe she *was* too quiet.

Maybe she needed to play the game better.

But then something shifted.

She realised she didn't need to become someone she wasn't.

She just needed to **stop hiding her impact.**

So, she started doing something simple, but powerful:

She spoke up more. She claimed her contributions.

Not to brag-but to stop disappearing.

She didn't shout. She didn't pretend.

She just started showing up with her full self.

Six months later, she led a project that changed the team's performance.

Not because she pushed others down-

But because she finally stopped minimizing herself.

It is Okay to Want More

There is nothing wrong with wanting to rise.

Wanting to be seen.

Wanting to be trusted with more.

That doesn't make you ungrateful.

That makes you human.

And if you are in a space where they keep underestimating you-

Don't let their short-sightedness become your self-worth.

You are allowed to grow even when no one claps.

You are allowed to want more, even when they say, "Be patient."

You are allowed to define your value, even when they don't.

Don't Shrink to Fit Their Comfort

If they only celebrate a certain kind of leader-

one who's louder, acts more polished, more predictable-when they are unsure,

that is not a reflection of your value.

That is a reflection of their limits.

You don't need to shrink to fit their expectations.

You don't need to wait for permission to grow.

You just need to remember:

You were never meant to stay small.

Let This Be Your Reminder:

"They might delay your progress-

but they can't cancel your purpose."

Keep going.

Keep growing.

And if the room doesn't see you?

Build your own table.

Or better yet-walk into the next one knowing exactly who you are.

They didn't notice every step you took,

or how much courage each one took.

But you kept going, heart in hand-

becoming more than they'd understand.

You are not late, and you are not lost-

you are learning things that matter most.

Your light was never theirs to name-

it's yours to carry, just the same.

Reflection Journal: Chapter 15– When They Try to Define Your Limits

*"They don't get to write your story-**you** do."*

1. Let It Out: What Did You Want to Hear?

Think back to a moment when someone downplayed your potential-at work, in school, in life.

- What did they say (or not say) that stuck with you?

- What did you *wish* they had said?

That moment felt like...

...

I wish someone had told me...

2. Own Your Quiet Progress

Recognition or not-you've grown. You've evolved.

List 2–3 ways you have grown that no one may have clapped for, but that you are proud of anyway.

Even if no one noticed, I am proud that I...

- ...
- ...
- ...

3. Unpack the Ceiling

Sometimes it's external limits. Sometimes it's our own fear.

What's one area where you have been playing smaller than you need to?

(And why do you think that is?)

I've been holding back in...

...

Because I've been afraid of...

...

4. Redefine Your Voice

Visibility doesn't have to mean being loud or fake.

It means being **clear.**

Being **seen** on your terms.

What's one way you can start showing your value-without changing who you are?

(Even a small habit counts.)

I can start by...

5. Build Your Space

If the current environment isn't seeing your worth... maybe it's time to stop waiting for their permission.

What would it look like to build a space-mentally, emotionally, professionally-where you feel seen, valued, and real?

In my ideal space, I would feel...

...

Gentle Reminder

"Just because they missed your light doesn't mean you stopped shining."

You're still becoming. And your worth was never up for debate.

Chapter 16: Become the Person You Needed

Because someone out there needs the version of you that never gave up.

Think back to a moment when you felt lost. Small. Overwhelmed.

What did you need most in that moment?

Maybe it was someone to believe in you.

Maybe it was a role model who looked like you.

Maybe it was a kind word, a hand to hold, or just someone saying,

"You are not crazy for wanting more."

Now here's the powerful truth:

You can become that person-for yourself and for others.

Think of it like inertia—once you start moving, you become the proof that staying in motion matters. Except unlike physics class, you don't need a push from a teacher throwing a ball across the room to get going, hehehe.....

The Pain You have Felt Has a Purpose

We often try to hide our scars-our past failures, insecurities, heartbreaks.

But those same wounds?

They are the reason you understand struggle.

They are the reason your voice has depth.

And when you rise from something difficult,

you carry wisdom that someone else desperately needs to hear.

You don't have to be perfect.

You just have to be real.

Aarav, Full Circle

Two years after Aarav's shaky pitch and slow comeback, he got invited to mentor students at a local business school. One of the organizers had followed his journey online-his ups, his honest posts about failing, and how he built back, one step at a time.

Aarav almost declined. "I'm still figuring it out," he said.

But then he remembered himself, sitting in the back row at a college event, desperately hoping someone would say: *"It's okay to be unsure. Just start anyway."*

So, he showed up. Not as someone who had it all figured out, but as someone who *stayed in the game* when it got hard. He spoke about rejection, about doubt, about the days with zero likes or funding.

After the session, a student came up to him and whispered,

"I thought I was the only one feeling stuck. But now I feel like maybe... I can keep going."

That's when it clicked for Aarav:

All those hard days meant something.

Not just for him, but for someone else trying to hold on.

Lead with What You have Learned

You might not realize it, but right now, someone is watching how you move through the world.

A younger sibling. A quiet coworker. A stranger who sees your posts.

They are not looking for flawless.

They are looking for **honest.**

Be the kind of person who shows up even when it is hard.

Who keeps going even when it is messy.

Not because you have all the answers,

but because you have chosen not to give up.

Turn Your Story into a Signal

The version of you who struggled to speak up?

The one who second-guessed everything?

The one who didn't know where to begin?

They are still part of you.

And they can still guide you.

Instead of pushing those versions away, bring them with you-

and let them remind you why this journey matters.

Not just for you,

but for everyone watching in silence, wondering if they can make it too.

Give What You Needed

If you needed encouragement, give it freely now.

If you needed belief, become someone who sees potential in others.

If you needed space to grow, create that space in your life-for yourself and for those around you.

You didn't get here easily.

So don't waste the rise.

Let it mean something.

Let it ripple.

Become the person you once needed-

and the world needs now.

Be who you needed when you felt alone-
the voice, the hand, the steady tone.
The one who says, "You'll find your way,"
and stays beside you when skies go grey.
You have lived the questions, felt the ache-
now you are the light someone else will take.
Not perfect, no-but real somehow.
The person you needed... and the world needs now.

Reflection Journal: Chapter 16– Become the Person You Needed

This chapter invites you to turn your struggles into strength-not just for yourself, but for someone else who might be walking the road you have already travelled.

1. Think back to a version of yourself who was struggling.

What did you need in that moment-support, direction, belief, space? Describe it.

2. How have you grown since then?

Lists the strengths, lessons, or values you've developed as a result of that struggle.

3. Who in your life today might be going through something similar?

Write down one person (or group) you could uplift with your story, presence, or support.

4. What would it look like to become the person *you* once needed?

☐ Be more patient

☐ Offer encouragement

☐ Share my story honestly

☐ Create safe spaces

☐ Other: ______________________________

5. What part of your journey are you still hiding or ashamed of-that could actually help someone else feel less alone?

Be honest. Sometimes, what we think makes us weak is what actually makes us relatable.

6. What's one thing you will do this week to let your story ripple outward?

It could be a conversation, a post, a small act of kindness, or simply showing up for someone.

"Your rise isn't just for you-it's for everyone who will rise because of you."

Chapter 17
The Quiet Power of Belief

Because belief doesn't have to be loud to change everything.

Let's be honest: it is hard to believe in yourself when you have been doubted, dismissed, or made to feel like you don't have what it takes.

Sometimes the world doesn't hand you encouragement.

Sometimes you don't have a cheer squad.

Sometimes your own mind becomes the loudest critic in the room.

But here's what I have learned-belief doesn't have to be big or bold.

It just has to be real.

A whisper is enough to begin.

"Maybe I can."

"Maybe I am not as far behind as I think."

"Maybe this version of me is enough to start."

Aarav's belief was built through action-by staying in the game, even when he couldn't see the finish line. But belief doesn't always begin with movement. Sometimes, it begins with a whisper. A quiet choice to try.

That's where Ishita's story begins.

Think of belief like a chain reaction in physics—one tiny spark, like a single neutron hitting a nucleus, can start an energy burst big enough to change everything

Belief Isn't Magic-It's a Muscle

Most people think self-belief is something you are born with. It's not.

It is something you build-slowly, like a muscle, through repetition.

Every time you do something you thought you couldn't...

Every time you show up on a day when it would have been easier to give up...

Every time you take the next step even when you are scared...

You grow it. Quietly. Steadily. Authentically.

Ishita's First Step

When Ishita moved from a small town to the city for college, everything overwhelmed her.

The pace. The people. The pressure.

In class, she barely spoke. Everyone seemed smarter, more confident, more... ready.

She almost dropped out after the first semester.

Not because she wasn't capable-

but because she had convinced herself she didn't belong.

One day, while walking back from campus, she saw a notice for an open mic night.

She loved writing poetry but had never shared it out loud.

Her first instinct was to ignore it.

But then she heard it-

A whisper: "*What if you just try?*"

That night, her hands trembled, her voice cracked-but she read her poem.

No standing ovation. No viral moment.

Just one girl in the back who came up later and said,

"Your words sounded like what I feel every day. Thank you."

That moment didn't launch a career.

It launched belief.

Today, Ishita hosts that same open mic, helping shy students find their voices.

Not because she became fearless-

but because she gave that whisper a chance to grow.

You Don't Have to Be Fully Confident-Just Willing

There is a myth that belief means you are100% sure everything will work out.

But belief is braver than that.

Belief is saying:

"I don't know how this ends. But I am willing to try anyway."

It is trusting that you are worth the effort.

That your dream matters.

That even if you fail, you will still be proud for trying.

That's real confidence.

The kind that doesn't need attention-just intention.

The World Reflects What You Radiate

Here's the thing: when you start to believe in yourself-even a little-other people feel it.

You Walk differently. Speak differently. Show up differently.

People treat you the way you treat yourself.

So, when you stop apologizing for taking up space,

when you stop shrinking your ideas to make others comfortable,

the world starts to adjust around your growth.

You Are Already Enough to Begin

You don't need to wait until you're "healed" or "ready" or "better."

You can begin with what you have.

Who you are right now is enough.

And if that little voice inside you has ever whispered,

"I think I could do something more..."

Please listen to it.

That is your future self-calling you forward.

Believe in your ability to figure it out.

Believe in the value of your voice.

Believe that the small steps count.

You don't need everyone to believe in you.

You just need to stop being the one who doesn't.

Reflection Journal: Chapter 17– The Quiet Power of Belief

You don't have to shout your dreams from the rooftops. But you do have to believe in them-just enough to take one step. Let this page be your space to listen to that whisper inside you.

1. What's something I deeply want to do or become-but haven't fully believed I could?

Be honest. No filters. What dream keeps tugging at you?

2. What's been holding me back from fully believing in myself?

☐ Fear of failure

☐ Comparison to others

☐ Lack of confidence

☐ Past mistakes

☐ Other: ______________________________

3. When have I surprised myself by doing something I thought I couldn't?

Even if it was small-write it down. You've done it before.

4. What's one belief I want to strengthen about myself starting today?

Example: "I believe I can speak up." / "I believe I deserve a seat at the table."

5. Who or what helps remind me of my strength when I forget?

A person, a memory, a quote, a moment-describe it.

6. What's one quiet step I can take this week to grow my belief muscle?

Try something new? Speak in class? Share your work online? Say "yes" to something that scares you just a little?

"It starts with a whisper.

A 'maybe I can.'

And from there-you rise."

Chapter 18: The Progress You Can't Post

Because some of your biggest wins will never fit in a caption.

Let's be honest-

We live in a world that loves quick wins and clean stories.

We are taught to measure success in numbers, likes, job titles, and milestones.

And when you don't have those things-

when the growth is slower, messier, or internal-

it can start to feel like you are not moving at all.

But here's the truth:

Some of the most powerful progress happens quietly.

There is no audience.

No applause.

Just you, doing the hard work of changing.

Think of it like a black hole gaining mass—on the outside, nothing looks different, but inside, an enormous amount of energy is building up. Quiet progress can be just as powerful—it just hasn't gone supernova yet!

Not All Growth Is Measurable

You can't post the fact that you didn't spiral this time.

That you stopped apologizing for your boundaries.

That you asked a question in a meeting you used to stay silent in.

That you finally sent the email. Or said no. Or said yes.

But those moments?

They are huge.

They are the quiet victories that rebuild your self-respect.

The small pivots that lead to big shifts.

The stuff that changes you, not just your feed.

Luca's Invisible Win

Luca worked in consulting-a world that thrived on performance and polish.

He hit targets. Delivered results.

But inside, he was burning out.

The kind of burnout that didn't show in spreadsheets-

just in short breaths and sleepless nights.

One day, after yet another 12-hour stretch of smiling through meetings,

he reached his limit.

He didn't quit his job.

He didn't launch something new.

He did something smaller-but braver.

He booked therapy.

He started journaling.

He set one boundary: no work emails after 9 PM.

It felt like nothing.

No one noticed.

But for the first time in years, **he noticed himself.**

A few months later, his manager told him,

"You are showing up differently these days. More grounded."

Luca smiled.

That was the win:

Becoming someone he respected again.

The World May Not See It-But You Will

There is growth that's visible to everyone-

a promotion, a launch, a move.

And then there's the kind that only you know:

- Getting back up after a quiet failure.

- Being kind to yourself on a bad day.
- Choosing patience when you'd usually panic.

It all counts.

Even when no one claps.

Stop Measuring Worth by Visibility

If you are only validating your progress when it's public,

you will miss the magic that's happening inside.

You don't need to perform your growth.

You don't need to prove your healing.

You just need to keep going.

Keep becoming.

Keep showing up for a life that feels like yours-even if no one's watching.

Redefine Success for Yourself

What if success wasn't a single moment to chase-

but a quiet, daily alignment with who you want to be?

What if progress was:

- Being proud of how you handled something hard?
- Taking care of your energy, not just your goals?

- Trusting the season you are in, even if it's slow?

Let that be enough today.

Gentle Reminder:

You don't owe the world proof of your progress.

The fact that you are still trying? Still growing? Still here?

That is more than enough.

And it matters-deeply.

Still Here

No medals hung, no spotlight glow,

Just quiet steps where few will go.

No need to prove how far you've come-

The fact you're here? That says you've won.

Reflection Journal: Chapter 18: The Progress You Can't Post

1. What have you done lately that no one saw-but took real strength?

(Maybe it was getting out of bed on a hard day. Setting a boundary. Saying no. Starting again.)

2. What are three small wins you have had this month that didn't come with applause—but mattered to you?

3. Are you giving yourself enough credit for the ways you are showing up?

What's one way you can affirm yourself more often?

4. When do you find yourself measuring your worth by external validation?

What can you remind yourself of in those moments?

5. If no one could see your progress, what would *you* still want to grow in?

What kind of progress feels meaningful to you-whether or not it's visible?

6. What are you proud of yourself for right now-even if no one else knows about it?

Write to yourself like you would a friend who's quietly doing the work.

Close With This:

Write a kind note to yourself.

"I am proud of you for..."

"You have come a long way since..."

"Even when it doesn't feel like much, I see how you..."

Chapter 19
Let Go to Level Up

Because sometimes the only thing standing between you and your next chapter-is what you are still holding on to.

We talk a lot about growth.

About becoming.

About chasing the dream.

But what we don't talk about enough...

is what you might need to leave behind to get there.

Not everything-and not everyone-is meant to come with you.

And that is hard to hear.

But it is also freeing.

Think of it like a rocket shedding its boosters–if it tried to carry everything to space, it would never escape gravity. Sometimes, to rise higher, you need to let go of what got you off the ground.

Some Things Served You Once-But Not Anymore

There are habits, beliefs, stories, and people that helped shape you.

But now? Some of them might be keeping you stuck.

That voice in your head saying,

"You are not good enough."

"Play it safe."

"Don't stand out."

That version of you who is still trying to prove something to everyone?

You don't need her anymore.

Letting go doesn't mean erasing the past.

It means choosing not to be ruled by it anymore.

Ishita's Quiet Goodbye

After Ishita found her voice through poetry, people started noticing her in new ways.

Teachers asked her to lead. Friends sought her advice.

She was growing-but something kept tugging her backward.

It was her fear of disappointing people who once knew a quieter version of her.

The ones who said, *"You've changed."*

The friends who preferred her small.

The old voice that whispered, *"Don't get too loud, they won't like it."*

She tried to shrink again.

To make others comfortable.

To stay relatable.

But it hurt. Quietly, deeply.

One day, while journaling, she wrote a single line:

"I can't become who I am meant to be while staying who I was to please everyone."

That was her turning point.

She didn't make a dramatic exit.

No big announcement.

Just a slow shedding of roles that no longer fit.

She stopped apologizing for her growth.

She started choosing spaces where she didn't have to dim to be accepted.

Letting go wasn't easy.

But it made room for something better-

her true self, in full bloom.

You Can't Take Flight Carrying Everyone's Baggage

Sometimes we stay small to stay accepted.

We keep relationships that drain us because they are familiar.

We hold onto identities that no longer feel true-just to avoid discomfort.

But elevation requires separation.

If you want to level up, you need to create space-mentally, emotionally, spiritually.

That means saying no.

That means grieving certain versions of your old self.

That means letting go, so you can finally rise with less weight.

This Isn't Abandonment. It's Alignment.

Letting go isn't about cutting off everything and everyone.

It is about asking:

"Does this thought, relationship, habit, or belief support who I am becoming?"

If the answer is no...

then you are allowed to gently set it down and move forward.

This is your permission slip:

You're allowed to outgrow people, patterns, and places.

Letting Go Makes Room for What's Meant for You

When your hands are full of what no longer fits,

you have no space to receive what actually aligns.

So, release the fear that says,

"What if I lose too much?"

And lean into the trust that says,

"What if I make room for something better?"

Because the next level of you isn't built by holding tighter.

It is built by letting go-with love, clarity, and courage.

Reflection Journal: Chapter 19: Let Go to Level Up

1. What are you currently holding onto that feels heavy or misaligned?

(This could be a belief, a habit, a relationship, a role, or even a self-expectation.)

2. Is there a version of yourself that you have outgrown, but still feel pressure to maintain?

Why? What would happen if you stopped performing that version?

3. Have you ever stayed small or silent to make others comfortable?

How did that feel in your body, in your spirit?

4. What's one thought or narrative you have carried for a long time that no longer serves your growth?

What might it sound like to replace it with something more empowering?

5. Who or what are you afraid of disappointing if you grow or change?

Is that fear rooted in love, or in expectation?

6. What space could open up in your life-mentally, emotionally, spiritually-if you gently let go of what no longer fits?

What might you be able to say yes to, once you say no to what's holding you back?

7. Finish this sentence:

To rise into the next version of me, I need to let go of...

A Grounding Affirmation:

"Letting go doesn't mean I have failed. It means I am listening to who I am becoming."

Chapter 20
Chase Progress, Not Perfection

Because you don't need to get it perfect-you just need to keep going.

Let's be real: perfection is a lie.

It is a moving target. A mirage. A standard you will never fully meet.

But still, so many of us chase it.

We wait until we are "ready," until it is polished, until we have all the answers.

We rewrite, rehearse, revise.

And in the process, we delay our dreams.

Why? Because we are afraid.

Afraid to look messy. To be judged. To fail publicly.

But guess what?

Progress doesn't care if it is messy-it just needs to be real.

You Don't Need to Be Great to Start

You have heard this before. But have you actually believed it?

We tell ourselves:

"Once I feel confident, I will begin."

"Once I get better, I will share it."

"Once it is perfect, I will hit post/submit/apply."

But that mindset traps you in a loop of never enough.

The truth?

You get better by doing-not by waiting.

From Ishita to Ayaan: Progress in Motion

Ishita's story of owning her voice had a ripple effect.

One of those ripples landed with **Ayaan**, a first-year engineering student who had been quietly following her open mic events online for months.

He was the kind of guy who filled notebooks with half-finished poems and startup ideas he never shared.

Every time he thought about posting or presenting, a voice in his head whispered:

"It's not good enough yet. Wait till you fix it."

But then he read one of Ishita's blog posts where she wrote:

"I'd rather be seen trying than never be seen at all."

That line stuck with him.

So, one evening, heart pounding, he signed up for the campus idea pitch night.

He stumbled through his intro. Fumbled with the slides.

It wasn't polished-but it was real.

And at the end, one of the faculty said,

"You're onto something. Don't stop."

That single comment lit a spark.

He didn't win that night-but he *started.*

And that progress?

It gave him more clarity, more courage, more energy than perfection ever had.

Now, Ayaan writes in public. Speaks at clubs. Iterates on the go.

His mantra?

"Done is better than perfect. Shaky is better than silent."

Perfection Kills Momentum

Perfectionism pretends to be ambition, but it is really fear in disguise.

It is fear of being seen in process.

Fear of being judged for not being there yet.

Fear of exposing your rough edges.

But your rough edges are where the growth happens.

That is where people relate to you.

That is where you start to believe:

"I don't have to do it flawlessly. I just have to do it fully."

After all, even the universe didn't get the Big Bang "perfect"– it was literally an explosion of chaos, and look how far we've come since then!

Small Wins Stack Over Time

You don't need a giant leap.

You just need one solid step today. And another one tomorrow.

That's how real change happens-in quiet, consistent, sometimes boring ways.

Celebrate the draft.

Post the imperfect idea.

Raise your hand, even if your voice shakes.

Every time you choose progress over perfection, you build momentum-

and momentum is magic.

You are Allowed to Evolve Out Loud

You are not supposed to have it all figured out.

You are supposed to grow. To refine. To learn on the way.

And when people watch you show up in the middle of the journey?

They are not judging you.

They are inspired by your courage to be seen.

So, keep moving. Keep learning.

You're not behind. You're becoming.

Reflection Journal: Chapter 20 – Chase Progress, Not Perfection

This journal isn't about doing it right. It's about doing it anyway. Show up as you are. You are allowed to figure it out on the way.

1. What's something I have been putting off because I am waiting for it to be "perfect"?

A project, a post, a decision, a conversation? Name it.

2. What am I actually afraid of?

☐ Being judged

☐ Looking unprepared

☐ Failing publicly

☐ Not meeting expectations

☐ Other: ______________________________

3. What's one small way I could make progress on it-today?

Think tiny step: write the first line, send the email, share the draft, ask the question.

4. Who inspires me by showing up *before* they were perfect? What can I learn from them?

It could be a friend, creator, athlete, or even Ayaan or Ishita.

5. What would I say to a friend stuck in perfectionism?

Now say it to yourself-with the same kindness.

6. What would it feel like to give myself permission to be "in progress"?

Visualize it. Describe it in your words. Freedom? Relief? Creativity?

"You don't need to get it right the first time.

You just need to get started."

Progress is a path. And you're already on it.

Chapter 21
Keep Showing Up

Because consistency-not brilliance-is what moves you forward.

Let's get one thing straight:

You don't need to have an amazing day to make it count.

You don't need to be at your best every single time.

You just need to keep showing up.

That's it.

Some days will feel electric. You'll feel focused, motivated, buzzing with ideas.

Other days? You'll feel like a slow, sluggish version of yourself.

And on those days, you might be tempted to check out. To say, "Not today."

But that's exactly when showing up matters most.

Because progress isn't made only on the good days.

It is made in the *ordinary* ones.

The tired ones. The "I don't feel like it" ones.

The days when you show up *anyway*.

You Don't Have to Crush It-You Just Have to Be There

We glorify "breakthroughs"-but the truth is, they're built on countless moments no one claps for.

The early morning when you rewrote that draft-again.

The night you sent the application with a shaky voice.

The walk you took when you didn't have the energy to run.

It all counts. It all stacks.

Because what you are really doing isn't just ticking off tasks-

You are building self-trust.

Every time you show up, you are proving to yourself:

"I am someone who follows through."

"I am someone who doesn't quit just because it's hard."

"I am building something-even if I can't see it fully yet."

And that? That's where transformation begins.

Ishita's Story: The Power of Showing Up

Ishita never imagined herself on a stage. Not even a small one.

She was the quiet kind. The one who wrote poems in the margins of notebooks but never let anyone read them.

After college, she joined a corporate job that paid the bills-but slowly chipped away at her confidence. Her creativity went quiet. Her voice? Even quieter.

But something shifted the day she accidentally walked into an open mic event during a solo weekend outing.

People were reading poems. Real, raw, imperfect.

Some stumbled. Some shook. But they still showed up.

She went home that night and dug out her oldest notebook. Pages filled with emotions she had buried.

She didn't get on stage the next day. Or even the next week.

But she made herself a promise: *just show up.*

She started attending the open mics silently-week after week-never reading, just listening.

Eventually, she scribbled her name on the sign-up sheet. Her voice trembled. Her hands shook. But she read. And people listened.

That was two years ago.

Today, she's hosted dozens of open mics, built a quiet but powerful online community for writers, and-most importantly-found her voice again.

It didn't happen all at once. It happened one awkward, uncertain, brave evening at a time.

You Never Know Who You're Inspiring

Here's the wild part:

While you are doubting yourself, someone else is watching you and feeling brave.

Your small steps-your vulnerable shares, your quiet consistency-might be the exact thing someone else needs to believe they can try, too.

Ishita didn't know her story would ripple into Ayaan's (remember the earlier Chapter ?).

But it did.

Because real progress? It's contagious.

It gives others permission to start-even when they feel far from ready.

Progress Loves Patience

You won't always see the results right away.

But that doesn't mean it is not working.

You are rewiring habits. Building resilience. Creating something real.

That kind of growth? It's slow, quiet, and often invisible... until it's not.

So, on the days it feels pointless-remember:

This is the work.

This is the becoming.

This is how you rise.

A Note to You

You don't have to move fast.

You don't have to be brilliant.

You don't even have to feel confident every day.

You just have to keep showing up.

That's how books get written.

That's how businesses are built.

That's how confidence is earned.

That's how lives change.

Not in one grand moment-but in a thousand quiet ones.

Kind of like how water dripping steadily can carve through rock over years–slow, consistent force can beat instant impact... even physics agrees!

Reflection & Journal Page

For Chapter 21: Keep Showing Up

1. When was the last time you showed up-*even when it was hard*?

Write about that moment. What did it teach you about yourself?

2. What area of your life needs more consistent action-even if it's small?

Name it. Don't overthink it. Just one honest area.

3. Define Your "Minimum Daily Move"

What's one tiny thing you can commit to doing daily that aligns with your goal?

→ I will: ___________________________ (Ex: Write for 10 mins. Walk for 15. Reach out to 1 person.)

5. A Note for Tough Days

Write a short reminder you can come back to when you want to give up.

→ "I may not see it yet, but I'm building something. And I will keep showing up because..."

Chapter 22
Stay With the Work

Because the real magic happens when you stay steady, not perfect.

We love to talk about passion.

About chasing dreams, taking bold steps, starting new things.

But what we don't always talk about is what comes next. The middle.

The not-so-glamorous, often messy, always humbling stretch of time where the excitement fades...

and you are left with the work.

No finish line in sight. No "likes" flooding in. No clear sign that you're even getting it right.

Just you. And the decision to stay with it.

This Is Where Most People Quit

Not because they are weak.

Not because they don't care.

But because focus takes effort in a world that profits off your distraction.

Discipline is hard.

Especially when no one is watching.

Especially when progress feels slow and invisible.

But here's what separates those who build something real from those who only talk about it:

They stay with the work-even when it is boring.

Even when it is hard.

Even when motivation is nowhere to be found.

No, It is Not Always Fun

Focus isn't about being constantly inspired.

It is about returning-again and again-to what matters.

It is about learning how to say, "Not now," to what looks urgent but isn't.

And instead saying, "These matters more."

It's not glamorous.

It's not attention-grabbing.

It's simply the quiet strength of choosing one thing and giving it your all.

Naomi's Story: The Work Behind the Vision

Naomi was known for starting things.

New business ideas. Side projects. Challenges. Vision boards.

But none of them stuck-because she moved on the moment it got hard or quiet.

One day, her coach asked her a simple question:

"What would happen if, instead of chasing the next shiny thing... you stuck with one?"

She didn't love that question.

But she picked one idea: a handmade journal brand built around self-reflection.

And for the first time, she committed to doing just that-no shortcuts, no switching lanes.

She gave herself six months.

The first few weeks? Pure adrenaline.

The next few? Doubt. Resistance. Boredom.

But Naomi didn't quit this time.

She made a habit of protecting time.

She wrote when she didn't feel like it.

She edited. Researched. Rewrote.

Some days, she only managed 15 minutes. But she kept showing up.

It was like charging a capacitor in physics—tiny efforts stacked slowly, but over time, they built enough "charge" to power something meaningful.

Six months later, her first product launched.

Not with a bang-but with clarity. With pride. With depth.

Because this time, she didn't just flirt with a dream.

She stayed with it long enough to bring it to life.

You Don't Need to Do More-You Need to Do Less, Better

The world tells you to do everything. Hustle harder. Multitask.

But focus says, "Do one thing. And do it with care."

Discipline doesn't mean grinding 24/7.

It means protecting what matters most-and letting the rest wait.

Want to finish your novel? Turn off the noise and write one messy page a day.

Want to build your health? Show up even when it's not your best workout.

Want to grow your craft? Spend 30 quiet minutes practicing, with no audience but yourself.

That is the path most people won't take.

But it is the one that works.

A Gentle Reminder:

You won't always feel like doing the thing.

But the discipline is in showing up anyway.

Focus is not a feeling- it is a choice.

Discipline is not punishment-it is devotion to your future self.

And in a world that wants you scattered and reactive...

your quiet commitment is rebellion.

And freedom.

The Work That Builds You

You won't always want to.

Some days, the page stays blank,

the steps feel heavier,

and your dream feels far away.

You'll be tempted to scroll, to wait, to wish.

But here's what you'll learn, slowly:

discipline isn't about being a machineit's about coming back to what matters,

even with tired hands and a quiet heart.

Not because the world is watching.

But because you are.

Each time you show up,

even with shaky focus or low energy,

you're saying:

"I'm still in this.

I still believe it's worth building."

And that builds something, too

not just the dream,

but the version of you

who no longer gives up on herself.

Think of it like half-life in physics—the effort might feel like it's decaying slowly, but as long as you keep showing up, there's always energy left to keep the process going!

Reflection Journal: Chapter 22: *Staying with the Work*

1. What's something you started with excitement but struggled to stay consistent with?

(Be honest–there is no shame in stopping. The insight lives in the why.)

→

2. What distractions tend to pull your focus away from what really matters to you?

(Are they digital? Emotional? Social? Internal?)

→

3. What would it look like to protect time for the one thing you care about—even just 15 minutes a day?

→

4. Finish the sentence:

"If I stayed with the work-even imperfectly-for the next 3 months, I might surprise myself by..."

→

5. Think of a time you followed through on something, even when it was hard. What did that build inside you?

→

6. What's one small thing you can do this week to move forward, without waiting to feel 'ready' or 'motivated'?"

→

Grounding Affirmation:

"I don't need perfect days. I need present ones. I can do small things with deep commitment."

Chapter 23
Own the Journey

Because getting their matters-but who you become along the way matters even more.

We talk a lot about "making it."

Getting the job. Launching the dream. Hitting the big moment.

But truthfully?

The most meaningful part of this whole thing isn't where you end up.

It is how you get there.

It is the quiet mornings when no one sees you trying.

It is the nights you keep going even though your heart is heavy.

It is every small decision you made to stay in the game-even when you wanted to quit.

That is the journey.

And that is where the becoming happens.

Starting From Nowhere

When **Elena** left home and flew to a new country with just one suitcase and a scholarship letter, she wasn't chasing fame or some perfect version of success.

She just wanted a chance. A fresh page.

Back home, life had felt like a dead end-family stress, money pressure, and a constant feeling that she didn't quite measure up.

She wasn't bold when she arrived.

She was scared. Homesick. Exhausted. But quietly determined.

The early months were brutal.

The accent felt foreign in her mouth. Everyone seemed faster, smarter, surer of themselves.

She worked double shifts just to stay afloat-café by night, tutoring by weekend, lectures in between.

She failed one of her first exams. Her professor said her writing was "too emotional."

That night, she didn't fall apart-she wrote through it.

Tried again. Bit by bit, she kept going.

Progress Doesn't Always Look Like Winning

Progress came in the tiniest moments:

Like when she didn't need to rehearse her sentences anymore.

When she asked a question in class without her heart racing.

When her younger sister back home said, "You sound stronger now."

No applause. No awards.

Just quiet wins. Small signs that she was growing.

And with time, she didn't just tolerate the struggle-she began to respect it.

Because every awkward day, every lonely night, every stumble had shaped her.

She wasn't just surviving anymore.

She was becoming.

You are Allowed to Be Proud Before You Arrive

By the time graduation came, yes-she was proud of the degree.

But even more? She was proud of the woman she had become.

The one who stayed.

The one who grew.

The one who stopped asking for permission and finally started trusting herself.

And What About You?

Maybe you are in that middle space right now.

Still figuring it out. Still building.

Still wondering if this part of your story even counts.

It does. So much more than you know.

You don't need the spotlight to make this season valuable.

You don't need a finish line to be proud of how far you have come.

The truth is-

If you can find pride, patience, and grace in the process itself...

you'll never need the outside world to validate your growth.

This Journey Wasn't a Detour-It Was the Way Forward

We want milestones. We want wins. We want certainty.

But sometimes, the most important work happens in the quiet climb.

In the unanswered questions. In the uncertain middle.

That's where you become someone unshakable.

So, keep going.

And don't rush to the summit.

Breathe. Look around. Own your steps-even the slow ones.

Because this is your story.

And it is not just about where you are going-

It is about who you've had the courage to become along the way.

You thought the rise would look like fireworks,

like crowds and cameras,

like a moment that made it all worth it.

But maybe it looked like this:

A morning you didn't quit.

A night you cried but still tried again.

A shaky voice that spoke up anyway.

Maybe it's not about arriving.

Maybe it's about staying–

when leaving would've been easier.

Loving the climb, not just the view.

Trusting yourself before the world ever claps.

You are not behind.

You are not late.

You are not unfinished.

You are becoming-

with every quiet step,

every uncertain try,

every breath that says:

"I am still here. I am still going."

Like how a glacier carves valleys over centuries—slow, steady, and powerful—even if no one notices the progress day to day.

And that?

That is what the journey was always for.

Reflection Journal: Chapter 23: *Owning Your Journey*

Take a quiet moment for yourself. Breathe deeply. You have come a long way-even if you haven't paused to notice it.

Use these prompts to reflect honestly, without pressure. This is for you.

1. What part of your journey have you been rushing through, and why?

→ What would happen if you slowed down and trusted the pace?

2. Think of a recent "small win" that you dismissed.

→ How did that moment actually show your growth or resilience?

3. Who have you become since you started this chapter of your life?

→ List a few ways you've changed-big or small.

4. What's one belief, fear, or old story you're ready to let go of as you move forward?

→ What are you ready to carry instead?

5. What would you say to the version of you who first began this journey?

→ Write it like a letter. Let it be kind.

You are allowed to be proud of how far you've come.

Not when it's perfect-right now, as it is.

Chapter 24
Finish Strong

Because how you end something says just as much as how you started it.

Starting is brave.

Showing up is powerful.

But finishing? That's rare.

Most people start strong and fizzle out when the excitement fades.

The newness wears off. The path gets longer. The results feel slower.

And that's when the doubt creeps in:

"Is this even worth it?"

"Why is this taking so long?"

"Maybe I am not cut out for this."

But here's the truth:

Every finish line you see was crossed by someone who felt exactly like that-and kept going anyway.

The Final Miles Are the Hardest-And the Most Important

The closer you get to your breakthrough, the heavier your legs might feel.

That is not weakness. That's momentum pressing forward.

Sometimes, finishing looks like:

- Getting up one more time than you fell
- Pushing through the awkward, quiet middle
- Holding your vision when no one else sees it yet

You don't need to feel on fire.

You just need to stay in motion.

Ayaan's First Finish Line

Ayaan had always been a starter.

New projects excited him. New ideas came easily.

But finishing? That was where he often lost steam.

His pitch night win gave him a boost-but the reality of following through hit harder than expected.

There were delays. Feedback that stung. Days when motivation vanished.

At one point, his college schedule clashed with everything.

He almost walked away.

"It's not working. Maybe I peeked too soon," he told himself.

But then he remembered what someone once told him:

"Anyone can be inspired. But it takes grit to keep going when no one's clapping anymore."

So, he did what most people don't:

He stayed.

He stopped chasing perfect and focused on *complete.*

He set deadlines-not for perfection, but for *progress.*

He worked in silent libraries, on messy whiteboards, in moments when no one else saw him grinding.

And when the final submission day arrived for the startup accelerator, Ayaan almost missed it-exhausted, sleep-deprived, unsure if it was even worth clicking send.

But he did.

And a week later, he got the email:

"Congratulations. You've made it to the next round."

It wasn't just about getting in.

It was about proving to himself that he could *finish* what he started.

He stood taller after that. Walked lighter.

Not because he had arrived-but because he hadn't abandoned himself halfway through.

No One Remembers the Perfect Start-They Remember the Powerful Finish

People won't remember if you were shaky at the beginning.

They'll remember that you showed up at the end-with integrity, with heart, with everything you had left.

Finishing strong doesn't mean finishing flawlessly.

It means finishing with intention. With purpose.

With the awareness that this chapter deserves to close with your full presence—not with your excuses.

The End is Just Another Beginning

When you finish something that mattered to you-whether it's a goal, a season, or even a healing process-you don't just get to feel proud.

You gain **proof**.

That you are capable.

That you followed through.

That you didn't quit when it got hard.

And that proof becomes fuel for what comes next.

Because there is always a next.

You are not done.

You are just **levelling up**.

So, take a breath.

Lift your head.

And finish strong.

Because even in physics, it's the final push–like the last bit of fuel that gets a rocket out of Earth's gravity–that makes all the difference.

Reflection Journal: Chapter 24– Finish Strong

Finishing doesn't mean perfection-it means presence. You have come this far. Let's help you cross that finish line.

1. What's something I started that I haven't yet finished?

Be honest. What's still open? A goal, a project, a dream, a healing process?

2. Why did I begin it in the first place?

Reconnect to your "why." What excited you? What did you hope to achieve, feel, or prove to yourself?

3. What's been getting in the way?

☐ Burnout

☐ Fear of failing

☐ Lack of clarity or motivation

☐ Life got busy

☐ Other: ______________________

4. What would finishing this mean to me now?

Would it give you closure? Confidence? A new beginning? Write the feeling you want.

5. What's one small action I can take this week to move closer to the finish line?

Send the email? Book the session? Pick up the phone? Open the draft? Start small, but start.

6. A note to myself, from my future self who finished it anyway:

Write a short message of encouragement from the version of you who didn't quit. What would they want you to hear today?

"Finishing isn't about having everything together.

It's about honouring what you started-

and proving to yourself that you're worth the follow-through."

Chapter 25
You Were the Rise All Along

Because the breakthrough you were chasing... was always you.

Let's pause for a second.

Look at how far you have come.

Maybe you didn't even realize it-because growth doesn't always feel like fireworks.

Sometimes it is just showing up on a Tuesday when your soul feels heavy.

Sometimes it is choosing honesty over ease.

Sometimes it is trying again, even after life knocked the wind out of you.

But here's what is true:

You didn't just rise-**you became the rise.**

The Rise Was Never About the Destination

You thought you were chasing a goal. A title. A version of success.

But what you were really doing was remembering who you are.

This whole time, you were:

- Learning how to trust yourself
- Choosing courage over comfort
- Letting go of what didn't fit anymore
- Building your voice, your habits, your path

You were becoming someone you could be proud of.

And **that is the real win.**

Ayaan, Beyond the Finish Line

After the bootcamp win, Ayaan expected clarity. Confidence.

But what came next was... silence again.

No offers flooded in.

No viral post.

Just life-quiet, steady, full of new uncertainties.

At first, he felt that familiar pull of self-doubt.

"Was that it? Was that my peak?"

"What if nothing bigger comes next?"

But then he caught himself-just in time.

Because this time, he was different.

He had lived through the valley. Climbed his own wall.

And **he had proof** now-of who he was *when no one was watching.*

So, Ayaan shifted focus.

He didn't chase another pitch. He **chose to give back.**

He started mentoring juniors who reminded him of himself two years ago-bright, unsure, full of messy ideas and questions.

He created a small online series called *"Build Before You're Ready"*-where he shared not the wins, but the *real story*:

- The nights he felt like quitting
- The times he presented without knowing all the answers
- The mornings he restarted from scratch with shaky hands

People listened.

Not because he was perfect. But because he was honest.

And in doing so, Ayaan realized something big:

He was no longer trying to rise.

He had already become the rise-for himself, and now, for others.

There Is No "After This"-There's Only Now

We live with this illusion that once we hit the goal, we'll finally feel "enough."

But enough-ness was never a destination you reached.

It was already in you-quiet, patient, waiting to be heard.

So don't wait for the world to validate you.

Don't wait for perfect timing, or a standing ovation, or the "right" version of you to show up.

Choose to rise now. As you are.

The Journey Isn't Over-It's Just Changed

This isn't an ending.

It's a **reintroduction**.

To yourself.

To your voice.

To your own power.

Now you carry something stronger than hype or hustle.

You carry **evidence**:

That you start things.

That you finish them.

That you keep going.

You don't need permission.

You don't need to play small anymore.

You have met the version of you that doesn't give up.

Hold on to her. She's your anchor.

You Were the Rise All Along

From day one, it was never about becoming someone else.

It was about returning to the truth that was already inside you:

You are **enough** to begin.

You are **strong enough** to continue.

You are **brave enough** to rise-again and again.

And now that you have started, don't stop.

Because someone out there is waiting to rise too—

and your story just lit the way.

Like resonance in physics–when one small vibration makes another object start moving too–you've become that resonant force for someone else.

Reflection Journal: Chapter 25– You Were the Rise All Along

This isn't the end. It's the beginning of a new way of seeing yourself.

Take a few quiet moments to reflect on everything you have lived, learned, and risen through.

1. What does "rising" mean to me now-after reading this book?

Has your definition of success, strength, or progress shifted? Write honestly.

2. In what small or quiet ways have I risen in the past year?

Growth isn't always loud. Did you keep going when no one noticed? Did you say yes-or no-when it mattered? Name those moments here.

3. What was one version of me I had to outgrow in order to rise?

That self deserves compassion. But you're no longer stuck in her story.

4. What do I now believe about myself that I didn't before?

Be bold. Be kind. Be true.

5. Who might need my story, my voice, or my encouragement right now?

Think of someone younger. Someone in your shoes. Someone who needs light. What would you say to them?

6. A final note to myself-to carry into whatever comes next:

Write a message from the version of you who now knows they are the rise. What do you want to remember on hard days? What truth will you return to?

"The rise wasn't a moment.

It was becoming someone I can believe in-again and again."

Chapter 26
This Is Your Chapter Now

Because maybe you didn't come this far just to be inspired-
maybe you came to remember who you are.

Let's take a breath for a second.

Not to rush to the end, but to feel what it means to have made it this far.

You have read stories.

You have seen parts of yourself on these pages.

You have nodded in quiet recognition.

You have paused. Maybe cried. Maybe even whispered, "*That's me.*"

And through it all-you stayed.

Not every chapter was easy.

Not every moment was a breakthrough.

But somehow, in the middle of life being loud, messy, unpredictable...

you stayed.

And that? That's powerful.

Like a star forging elements under immense pressure—you've been quietly shaping something stronger within you, even when no one could see it.

You Didn't Just Read This Book-You Lived It

No one gave you a manual on how to keep going when the world got heavy.

But you still found a way.

No spotlight. No finish line. No fanfare.

Just you, quietly choosing to keep showing up.

That is not weakness. That is strength in its rawest form.

This isn't about becoming someone brand new.

It is about remembering what's been true all along:

You are not broken.

You are not behind.

You are not too late.

You are *becoming.*

You Don't Need to Have It All Figured Out

Seriously, you don't.

You just need to keep choosing the next right thing.

Even if it is small. Even if your voice shakes. Even if you don't feel ready.

You have already done harder things than this.

So don't let one slow day convince you the journey doesn't matter.

Don't let someone else's timeline make you feel like you're falling behind.

What you are building? It is real.

What you are feeling? It is valid.

What you are carrying? It counts.

Think of a snowball rolling downhill—the more you stay in motion, the more power and weight your efforts gain over time.

So, What Now?

Now... you live.

Not for perfection. Not for productivity. Not for applause.

You live with intention.

You choose rest when you need it. You choose courage when you can.

You give yourself grace on the days it all feels too much.

You write the next chapter-not to impress anyone,

but because you've come too far not to keep going.

A Quiet Reminder to Take with You

The world might forget your small efforts.

But they matter.

The days you chose kindness over cynicism.

The mornings you got out of bed when your heart felt heavy.

The moments you kept hope alive when doubt was louder.

They matter. *You* matter.

This isn't just the end of a book.

It is the beginning of something honest.

And the pen?

It is in your hands now.

This is your chapter.

Go write it with your whole heart.

We'll be cheering from every page forward.

The next chapter? That one is yours to name.

Unwritten, unfiltered-waiting for your voice.

So go on, turn the page... the story is just beginning.

You're Still Becoming

You don't need to roar to prove you're strong.

Some days, survival *is* the song.

Not every step is bold or bright

But it's still a step. And that's still right.

You showed up tired. You showed up late.

You showed up doubting it was fate.

But you showed up. And that's the thread-

The quiet kind of brave we don't always get fed.

You've carried fear, and kept it near,

But walked ahead-year after year.

And if today feels soft or slow,

That's still becoming. That's still growth.

So, here's to the version of you that tries,

Even when the fire is just a spark in your eyes.

You've made it here. But this isn't done-

You're not at the end.

You've just begun.

Reflection Journal:26 Write Your Way Forward

These prompts aren't here for perfect answers.

They are here for honest ones.

Take your time. There is no rush.

1. What moment or chapter from this book felt like it was written *for* you? Why?

2. What version of yourself have you started to outgrow-and what are you stepping into?

3. In what small, ordinary ways are you already showing up for yourself? List them. Name them. Celebrate them.

4. Who are you becoming-on your own terms? Not for applause. Not for approval. Just for you.

5. Write a message to your future self. Be kind. Be honest. Remind yourself of what really matters.

Dear future me,

I hope you remember...

I hope you keep...

And even when it's hard, I hope you still...

Remember:

You don't need to have it all figured out.

You just need to keep walking with your eyes open,

your heart soft,

and your belief intact-even if it is quiet.

You were the rise all along.

And you still are.

Final Reflection / Farewell Letter

And This Is Where We Pause

A Note from Me to You

If you are holding this book near the end, I just want to say something simple-**thank you**.

Not for finishing every chapter, not for highlighting or underlining or nodding along.

But for sitting with yourself through the pages.

For staying.

For breathing deeper when something hit close to home.

For maybe pausing when it felt a little too real.

We don't always give ourselves credit for the quiet effort-

the effort of **trying to understand ourselves better,**

the effort of **changing gently,**

the effort of **not rushing the becoming.**

Books can't solve everything.

But if this one reminded you-**even once**-that your path is still yours to walk,

then I hope you will carry that knowing with you, even after you close the cover.

No pressure to have it all figured out.

No race. No timeline.

Just you-and the quiet strength it took to keep going.

You made space for yourself here.

And that is never small.

– Always in your corner,

Shabeena Mirza

"Don't Close the Book Yet"

Your Turn Now

Before you close this book-pause.

Take a moment.

Breathe.

Feel everything you have moved through-not just in these pages, but in your own life.

Now, flip to a fresh page in your journal.

Or grab a napkin. A sticky note. A notes app.

Whatever you have.

And write just one thing:

"This is where I begin..."

Because the next story that matters most?

It is not written here.

It is written by you.

Not with perfect grammar.

Not with a flawless plan.

But with real heart, clear intention, and the courage to begin again.

Like a photon finding its way,

your next step can light the day—it may feel small, but it carries the steady, honest spark of change that begins with you.

So go ahead-start messy. Start proud.

Just... start.

We are all waiting to read it.

"Write the Next Line"

One thing I want to remember from this book is...

The version of me I am becoming is...

My next small step looks like...

Final Quote Page

"You are not just a chapter-
you are the whole story still being written.
Keep the pen moving."

– Shabeena Mirza

About the Author

Shabeena Mirza is not a motivational speaker or a life guru-just someone who's been in the middle of the mess and chose to write through it. This book was born out of lived moments: the quiet battles, the self-doubt, the tiny wins, and the decision to keep going when giving up felt easier. It wasn't written from a mountaintop, but from the middle of the climb.

Writing this book was a journey of its own. There were days of clarity and nights filled with second-guessing. Pages got rewritten, stories shifted, and some chapters took longer than expected-because they were still being lived. But every word was shaped by truth, honesty, and the hope that someone, somewhere, would feel less alone in their becoming.

If you want to stay in touch, share your story, or just say hello, I'd love to hear from you.

Email: **shabeena.mirza46@gmail.com**

Let's keep walking this path-together.